THE OFFICIAL

WALT DISNEY

QUOTE BOOK

THE OFFICIAL

WALT DISNEY

QUOTE BOOK

COMPILED BY THE STAFF OF THE

WALT DISNEY ARCHIVES

EDITIONS

LOS ANGELES • NEW YORK

Editorial Director: **Wendy Lefkon**
Senior Editors: **Jennifer Eastwood and Jim Fanning**
Editorial Assistant: **Lori Campos**
Senior Designer: **Lindsay Broderick**
Managing Editor: **Monica Vasquez**
Production: **Anne Peters and Marybeth Tregarthen**

ISBN 978-1-368-06187-2
FAC-004510-23020

Printed in the United States
First Hardcover Edition, February 2023
10 9 8 7 6 5 4 3 2 1

Visit www.disneybooks.com

D23

THE OFFICIAL DISNEP FAN CLUB

CONTENTS

vii PREFACE

1 CHAPTER 1 on films and animation

41 CHAPTER 2 on Mickey Mouse

47 CHAPTER 3 on storytelling

59 CHAPTER 4 on the Disney theme parks

97 CHAPTER 5 on business and The Walt Disney Company

121 CHAPTER 6 on success and failure

133 CHAPTER 7 on money

147 CHAPTER 8 on children, young and old

173 CHAPTER 9 on family

179 CHAPTER 10 on education

199 CHAPTER 11 on America

207 CHAPTER 12 on animals and nature

223 CHAPTER 13 on art, music, and dance

231 CHAPTER 14 on progress and innovation

241 CHAPTER 15 on television

255 CHAPTER 16 on enlightenment, exploration, and experimentation

269 CHAPTER 17 on life

289 CHAPTER 18 on health and wellness

295 CHAPTER 19 on love, kindness, and peace

305 CHAPTER 20 on wonder

311 CHAPTER 21 on gratitude and appreciation

326 ACKNOWLEDGMENTS

328 SOURCES

340 IMAGE CREDITS

341 PHOTO CAPTIONS

PREFACE

DURING HIS LONG CAREER, WALT DISNEY frequently commented on his philosophies of life, his ideals, his dreams, and his hopes for a better world. This book is a collection of those quotations attributed to Walt. His words have been gleaned from publications, productions, and interviews over the breadth of his amazing career. Some are simple nuggets of homespun wisdom, while others are statements of deep insight gained while he crafted the enchanting films, television shows, and unparalleled experiences that are so beloved by audiences the world over.

Walt once said, "In order to make good in your chosen task, it's important to have someone you want to do it for. The greatest moments in life are not concerned with selfish achievements but rather with the things we do for the people we love and esteem, and whose respect we need." So this book is dedicated to the esteemed founder of the Walt Disney Archives, Dave Smith, who gathered and edited the first book of Walt's quotes and left us an incredible road map to follow.

It has been compiled for those whom we at the Walt Disney Archives are most grateful for . . . those discerning souls who are eager to learn more about the man who made such an incredible, positive impact on his own time and on the future yet to be— Walt Disney, the Showman of the World.

Rebecca Cline
Director, Walt Disney Archives
February 2023

CHAPTER 1

on films and animation

"**The motion picture has become a necessity of life,** a part of our balanced existence. It is not a negligible luxury. People are always going to demand and enjoy movies in the theater. Perhaps not as exclusively as they did when public amusements were more limited. Patronage will depend more than ever upon what we put on the screen. And especially on how well we understand the needs and desires of our younger customers. For their favor we must compete as never before."

"THE BUSINESS HAS GROWN CONTINUOUSLY THROUGH THESE YEARS, although at times the road was rocky. But I don't know of any other entertainment medium that can give to the millions of families the world over more value than the motion picture."

"SO, I TRIED TO GET A JOB IN HOLLYWOOD, working in the picture business so I could learn it. I would have liked to have been a director, or any part of that, but there was nothing open, so before I knew it I had my drawing board out and started back at the cartoon."

"I STARTED, ACTUALLY, TO MAKE MY FIRST ANIMATED CARTOONS IN 1920. Of course, they were very crude things then and I used sort of little puppet things."

"WELL, IN ORDER TO CRACK THE FIELD, I SAID, 'I've got to get something a little unique,' you see. Now they had the clown out of the inkwell who played with the live people. So I reversed it. I took the live person and put him into the cartoon field. I said, 'that's a new twist.' And it sold. I was surprised myself."

"PEOPLE STILL THINK OF ME AS A CARTOONIST, but the only thing I lift a pen or pencil for these days is to sign a contract, a check, or an autograph."

"TO CAPTIVATE OUR VARIED AND WORLDWIDE AUDIENCE OF ALL AGES, the nature and treatment of the fairy tale, the legend, the myth has to be elementally simple. Good and evil, the antagonists of all great drama in some guise, must be believably personalized. The moral ideals common to all humanity must be upheld. The victories must not be too easy. Strife to test valor is still and always will be the basic ingredient of the animated tale as of all screen entertainments."

"SPEAKING FOR THE ONE FIELD WHICH I FEEL definitely qualified to comment on, I fully believe the animated picture will emerge as one of the greatest mediums, not only of entertainment but also of education."

"ART IS NEVER CONSCIOUS. Things that have lived were seldom planned that way. If you follow that line, you're on the wrong track. We don't even let the word 'art' be used around the studio. If anyone begins to get arty, we knock them down. What we strive for is entertainment."

"THIS IS NOT 'THE CARTOON MEDIUM.' It should not be limited to cartoons. We have worlds to conquer here . . . we're doing beautiful things with beautiful music. We're doing comic things, fantastic things, and it can't be all the same— it's an experimental thing, and I'm willing to experiment on it. We've got more in this medium than making people laugh—we love to make people laugh, but I think we can do both. . . . the beauty we can get from controlled color and the music and everything we use here will be worth it . . . Excuse me if I get a little riled up on this stuff . . . It's going to take time to get ourselves up to the point where we can really get some humor in our stuff, rather than just belly laughs; and get the beauty in it, rather than just a flashy postcard. It takes time to do that, but I think we will . . ."

"To translate the world's great fairy tales, thrilling legends, stirring folk tales into visual theatrical presentations and to get back warm response of audiences in many lands has been for me an experience and a lifetime satisfaction beyond all value."

"Animation is different from other parts. Its language is the language of caricature. Our most difficult job was to develop the cartoon's unnatural but seemingly natural anatomy for humans and animals."

"ANIMATION CAN EXPLAIN WHATEVER THE MIND OF MAN CAN CONCEIVE. This facility makes it the most versatile and explicit means of communication yet devised for quick mass appreciation."

"I TAKE GREAT PRIDE IN THE ARTISTIC DEVELOPMENT OF CARTOONS. Our characters are made to go through emotions which a few short years ago would have seemed impossible to secure with a cartoon character. Some of the action produced in the finished cartoon of today is more graceful than anything possible for a human to do."

"To THINK SIX YEARS AHEAD—
EVEN TWO OR THREE—in this business of
making animated cartoon features, it takes
calculated risk and much more than blind faith
in the future of theatrical motion pictures. I see
motion pictures as a family founded institution
closely related to the life and labor of millions
of people. Entertainment such as our business
provides has become a necessity, not a luxury.
Curiously, it is the part which offers us the
greatest reassurance about the future in the
animation field. Fantasy, when properly done
in the one medium best adapted to its nature,
need never stale for the family taste."

"WE ARE NOT TRYING TO ENTERTAIN THE CRITICS.

I'll take my chances with the public."

"**MOVIE MAKERS ARE OFTEN TOO INTROVERTED ABOUT THEIR PRODUCTION.** They tend to build up myths about audiences and to prattle glibly about shifting public taste and its unpredictables. In considering audiences and our professional function, remember one thing: Americans are a sociable folk; we like to enjoy ourselves in crowds, at sports arenas, at picnics, fairs and carnivals, at concerts, and at the theater. Above all, we like to laugh together—even at our own shortcomings. I don't like to kid myself about the intelligence and taste of audiences. They are made up of my neighbors, people I know and meet every day. Folks I trade with, go to church with, vote with, compete in business with, help build and preserve a nation with."

"PUBLIC TASTE IN AMUSEMENT HAS CHANGED very decidedly since the early days when the motion picture was a toy, a novelty; it has changed as much in animation as in live-action cinema offerings."

"BEFORE SITTING DOWN TO COUNT MY BLESSINGS, I want to make you a promise. I promise we won't let this great honor you have paid us tonight go to our head—we have too many projects for the future to take time out for such a thing. On top of that, after forty-some-odd years of ups and downs in this crazy business of ours, we know too well—you are only as good as your next picture."

"FILMS STIMULATE CHILDREN
to read books on many subjects."

**"WE HAVE CREATED CHARACTERS
AND ANIMATED THEM** in the dimension
of depth, revealing through them to our
perturbed world that the things we have in
common far outnumber and outweigh
those that divide us."

"OUR FIELD OF ENTERTAINMENT STILL HAS MANY NEW and exciting and wonderful things to bring to the restless public wanting variety and novelty in the movie theater. The only thing we should fear and be on constant guard against is getting bogged down—getting into the ruts of monotony and timeworn repetitions which the business of entertainment cannot long stand."

"ALL CARTOON CHARACTERS
AND FABLES MUST BE EXAGGERATION,
CARICATURES. It is the very nature of
fantasy and fable."

"I TRY TO BUILD A FULL
PERSONALITY FOR EACH of our
cartoon characters—to make them
personalities."

"IN THESE EXTRAORDINARY DAYS WE REALIZE FULLY that the public is shopping more than ever for its box office fare. There is no compromise for 'selling' your attractions. I am confident that the future will enable us to fill this bill."

"MORE THAN ANY OTHER
MEDIUM, THE MOTION PICTURE is being
challenged to meet the greatly enlarged
opportunities and responsibilities of
modern showmanship."

"THROUGH HISTORICAL TIME—
AND EVEN AMONG OUR aboriginal
forefathers—all the races of man have
been dramatizing these eternal quests and
conquests of mind and heart; in arenas,
around tribal fires, in temples and theaters.
The modes of entertainment have changed
through the centuries; the content of public
shows, very little."

"LITERARY VERSIONS OF OLD FAIRY TALES ARE USUALLY thin and briefly told. They must be expanded and embellished to meet the requirements of theater playing time, and the common enjoyment of all members of moviegoing families. The screen version must perceive and emphasize the basic moral intent and the values upon which every great persistent fairy tale is found. To these ends I have devoted my own best efforts and the talents of my organization, in full realization of our responsibility as a mass entertainer and especially our responsibility to our vast audience of children around the world."

"REPORTERS ARE ALWAYS ANALYZING OUR APPROACH to entertainment, but there's no magic formula. I just make what I like—warm and human stories, and ones about historic characters and events, and about animals. If there is a secret, I guess it's that I never make the pictures too childish, but always try to get in a little satire of adult foibles. Also, we do everything our own way, for ourselves, with no outside interference. We stay close to the fundamentals of family entertainment and recreation, and have complete voice in the marketing."

"I WAS DOING THIS 'SORCERER'S APPRENTICE' with Mickey Mouse and I happened to have dinner one night with [Leopold] Stokowski. And Stokowski said, 'Oh, I'd love to conduct that for you.' . . . Well, that led to not only doing this one little short subject but it got us involved to where I did all of *Fantasia* and before I knew it I ended up spending four hundred and some odd thousand dollars getting music with Stokowski. But we were in then and it was the point of no return. We went ahead and made it."

"FANTASIA, TO ME, IS A WHOLE NEW OPPORTUNITY. For my medium it opens up unlimited possibilities. Music has always played a very important part since sound came into the cartoon. Now, the full expression that comes from the new Fantasound opens up a whole new world for us."

"IN THIS VOLATILE BUSINESS
OF OURS . . . we can ill afford to
rest on our laurels, even to pause in
retrospect. Times and conditions change
so rapidly that we must keep our aim
constantly focused on the future."

"WE ALLOW NO
geniuses around our studio."

"AFTER A LONG CONCENTRATION ON LIVE-ACTION AND CARTOON FILMS, we decided to try something that would employ about every trick we had learned in the making of films. We would combine cartoon and live-action in an enormous fantasy—*Mary Poppins*. And what a far cry that was from *Snow White*. As the original *Mary Poppins* budget of five million dollars continued to grow, I never saw a sad face around the entire studio. And this made me nervous. I knew the picture would have to gross ten million dollars for us to break even. But still there was no negative head-shaking. No prophets of doom. Even Roy was happy. He didn't even ask me to show the unfinished picture to a banker. The horrible thought struck me—suppose the staff had finally conceded that I knew what I was doing."

"CAUTION THERE MUST
BE, OF COURSE, along with
venturesome courage. The motion
picture business has long been
a chance-taking business. This
doesn't mean timidity in planning
an operation."

"BEFORE OUR EYES, WE HAVE
SEEN AN ENTIRE INDUSTRY GROW,
LITERALLY FROM THE GROUND UP.
And this growth was no accident. It was
painstakingly built, step by step, by men
with pioneering spirit who loved this
puzzling new art form . . . and believed
in its future."

"I HAVE EVERY CONFIDENCE THAT SO LONG AS OUR film presentations toughen the minds and warm the heart with the best, the motion picture industry can offer in art and craftsmanship and genuine human warmth, so long may we expect prosperous support and a long life."

"THE MOTION PICTURE WILL NEVER FULLY REPLACE THE PRINTED WORD, but it will go a long way in becoming its most valuable adjunct. There seems little question that the human mind will absorb picturized information much quicker than by means of the printed word."

"I THINK ONE REASON WHY PEOPLE LIKE OUR FILMS is that so much effort is made to give them adult as well as child appeal. Children laugh at entirely different things from those which amuse grown people. Where the subject matter is a little deep for children, amusing action must be injected to hold their interest."

"I AM NOT INFLUENCED BY THE TECHNIQUES or fashions of any other motion picture company."

"THE INSPIRATION OF MIND AND SPIRIT THAT GO INTO THE MAKING OF DISNEY PICTURE-MAKING—one essential is clarity. The other is interest; if he is shown that it relates directly to his needs, if he is made eager to learn and learning becomes—as it can be one of the keenest of pleasures; then he will learn far more readily and surely than if he is forced to drudge along under the whip of compulsion or duty. Failure to make clear the nature and meaning of the thing being produced is one of the surest causes of dullness and failure to learn. The success of our movies has sprung from their universal appeal to millions of people of all nations, all ages, all degrees of experience, intelligence and learning."

"THE MOTION PICTURE STILL
HAS GREAT THINGS AHEAD.
Equipped with its big screens, its
color and sound fidelities, and all its
perfected devices for illusionment,
nothing is beyond its range and powers.
Itself a marvel of science, it can and
will serve with equal facility the space
enthusiast looking beyond the sun,
and the homebody content with the
warm familiar earth and all its bounties
when he goes with his family seeking
entertainment and inspiration."

"THE SCREEN HAS TOO LONG BEEN CONFINED TO WHAT we can see and hear, what the camera can show . . . things which reveal not the half of a man's life and his most intense interests, with live actors attempting to interpret the unseen—the emotions, the impulses of the mind. And doing it, we must admit, rather clumsily most of the time. Relying largely on words often almost meaningless. Now, with the animated cartoon, we have another perfected tool—another scope—for getting at the inner nature of things and projecting them for the eye and the ear."

"I've NEVER BELIEVED IN DOING SEQUELS. I didn't want to waste the time I have doing a sequel; I'd rather be using that time doing something new and different. It goes back to when they wanted me to do more pigs."

"THE TRUTH OF THE MATTER IS THAT BY THE TIME we had the studio built, the banks owed me money, thanks to *Snow White*. And it gave me more personal satisfaction than anything I have ever done because it proved to a lot of sneering critics that a full-length cartoon could make money."

"THE SUCCESS OF THE SILLY
SYMPHONIES GAVE US the courage for
Snow White. And you should have heard
the howls of warning! It was prophesied
that nobody would sit through a cartoon
an hour and a half long. But we had
decided there was only one way we could
successfully do *Snow White*—and that was
to go for broke—shoot the works. There
could be no compromise on money, talent,
or time. We did not know whether the
public would go for a cartoon feature—but
we were darned sure that audiences would
not buy a bad cartoon feature."

"ANIMATED PICTURE-MAKING IS AN EXPENSIVE BUSINESS. One wrong pencil line can cost hundreds of dollars. I can't hold a pencil to the artists in my studio. I credit the success of my films to the teamwork in my organization."

"IN ALL MY YEARS OF PICTURE-MAKING I HAVE NEVER had more satisfaction or felt more useful in the business of entertainment than I have in making the True-Life Adventure features."

"WOMEN ARE THE BEST JUDGES OF ANYTHING WE TURN OUT. Their taste is very important. They are the theater-goers, they are the ones who drag the men in. If the women like it, to heck with the men."

CHAPTER 2

on Mickey Mouse

"ALL WE EVER INTENDED FOR HIM OR EXPECTED OF HIM was that he should continue to make people everywhere chuckle with him and at him. We didn't burden him with any social symbolism, we made him no mouthpiece for frustrations or harsh satire. Mickey was simply a little personality assigned to the purposes of laughter."

"THE LIFE AND VENTURES OF MICKEY MOUSE HAVE BEEN closely bound up with my own personal and professional life. It is understandable that I should have sentimental attachment for the little personage who played so big a part in the course of Disney Productions and has been so happily accepted as an amusing friend wherever films are shown around the world. He still speaks for me and I still speak for him."

"WE FELT THAT THE PUBLIC, AND ESPECIALLY THE CHILDREN, like animals that are cute and little. I think we are rather indebted to Charlie Chaplin for the idea. We wanted something appealing, and we thought of a tiny bit of a mouse that would have something of the wistfulness of Chaplin—a little fellow trying to do the best he could."

"WHEN PEOPLE LAUGH AT MICKEY MOUSE it's because he's so human; and that is the secret of his popularity."

"I ONLY HOPE THAT WE NEVER LOSE SIGHT OF ONE THING—that it was all started by a mouse."

"... THE STORY OF MICKEY is truthfully the real beginning of Disneyland."

CHAPTER 3

on storytelling

"THERE IS MORE TREASURE IN BOOKS THAN IN ALL THE PIRATES' LOOT ON TREASURE ISLAND and at the bottom of the Spanish Main . . . and best of all, you can enjoy these riches every day of your life."

"EVERYONE HAS BEEN REMARKABLY INFLUENCED BY A BOOK, OR BOOKS. In my case it was a book on cartoon animation. I discovered it in the Kansas City Library at the time I was preparing to make motion-picture animation my life's work. The book told me all I needed to know as a beginner—all about the arts and the mechanics of making drawings that move on the theater screen. From the basic information I could go on to develop my own way of movie storytelling. Finding that book was one of the most important and useful events in my life. It happened at just the right time. The right time for reading a story or an article or a book is important. By trying too hard to read a book that, for our age and understanding, is beyond us, we may tire of it. Then, even after, we'll avoid it and deny ourselves the delights it holds."

"CARTOON ANIMATION OFFERS A MEDIUM OF STORYTELLING and visual entertainment which can bring pleasure and information to people of all ages everywhere in the world."

"IN LEARNING THE ART OF STORYTELLING BY ANIMATION, I have discovered that language has an anatomy. Every spoken word, whether uttered by a living person or by a cartoon character, has its facial grimace, emphasizing the meaning."

"SHEER ANIMATED FANTASY IS STILL MY FIRST and deepest production impulse. The fable is the best storytelling device ever conceived, and the screen is its best medium. And, of course, animal characters have always been the personnel of fable; animals through which the foibles as well as the virtues of humans can best and most hilariously be reflected."

"UNTIL A CHARACTER BECOMES A PERSONALITY IT CANNOT BE BELIEVED. Without personality, the character may do funny or interesting things, but unless people are able to identify themselves with the character, its actions will seem unreal. And without personality, a story cannot ring true to the audience."

"IF I CAN'T FIND A THEME, I CAN'T MAKE A FILM ANYONE ELSE WILL FEEL. I can't laugh at intellectual humor. I'm just corny enough to like to have a story hit me over the heart."

"FROM YEARS OF EXPERIENCE
I HAVE LEARNED WHAT could
legitimately be added to increase the
thrills and delights of a fairy tale without
violating the moral and meaning of the
original. Audiences have confirmed this
unmistakably. We define the heroines and
heroes more vividly; add minor characters
to help carry the story line; virtually create
such immortal friends of the heroine as
the Seven Dwarfs. Storywise, we sharpen
the decisive triumph of good over evil
with our valiant knights—the issues which
represent our moral ideals. We do it in a
romantic fashion, easily comprehended by
children. In this respect, moving pictures
are more potent than volumes of familiar
words in books."

"AS A KID, I HAD SEEN THE STORY AND LIKED IT. The figures of the dwarfs intrigued me. I thought it was a good plot, and it had a broad appeal. It wasn't too fantastic. That's what you need: a fairly down-to-earth story that people can associate themselves with."

"IN OUR FULL-LENGTH CARTOON FEATURES, AS WELL AS IN OUR LIVE-ACTION PRODUCTIONS, we have tried to convey in story and song those virtues that make both children and adults attractive. I have long felt that the way to keep children out of trouble is to keep them interested in things. Lecturing to children is no answer to delinquency. Preaching won't keep youngsters out of trouble, but keeping their minds occupied will."

"**IN LIVE ACTION, YOU CAN TAKE A MEDIOCRE STORY** and put in interesting characters and personalities and have a good show. We can't do that in cartoons. We can't hire actors; we have to create them ourselves. We have to make them interesting or we're sunk. I've had a lot of fun making live-action pictures, mainly because I can move so fast. But I've learned a lot from them. I've made mistakes, but now I can apply the lessons to cartoons."

"FROM TIME TO TIME, WE TRY TO BRING YOU STRANGE AND UNUSUAL STORIES. I think the tale that I am about to relate is one of the most unusual that I have ever come across."

CHAPTER 4

on the Disney theme parks

"IT CAME ABOUT WHEN MY DAUGHTERS WERE VERY YOUNG and Saturday was always daddy's day with the two daughters. So we'd start out and try to go someplace, you know, different things, and I'd take them to the merry-go-round and I took them different places and as I'd sit while they rode the merry-go-round and did all these things—sit on a bench, you know, eating peanuts—I felt that there should be something built where the parents and the children could have fun together. So that's how Disneyland started. Well, it took many years . . . it was a period of maybe fifteen years developing. I started with many ideas, threw them away, started all over again. And eventually it evolved into what you see today at Disneyland. But it all started from a daddy with two daughters wondering where he could take them where he could have a little fun with them, too."

"DISNEYLAND WOULD BE A WORLD OF AMERICANS, past and present, seen through the eyes of my imagination—a place of warmth and nostalgia, of illusion and color and delight."

"WHEN I STARTED ON DISNEYLAND, [my wife] used to say, 'But why do you want to build an amusement park? They're so dirty.' I told her that was just the point— mine wouldn't be."

"DISNEYLAND IS LIKE ALICE STEPPING THROUGH THE LOOKING GLASS; to step through the portals of Disneyland will be like entering another world."

"A WORD MAY BE SAID IN REGARD TO THE CONCEPT and conduct of Disneyland's operational tone. Although various sections will have the fun and flavor of a carnival or amusement park, there will be none of the 'pitches,' game wheels, sharp practices and devices designed to milk the visitor's pocketbook."

"ON OUR FIRST TELEVISION PROGRAM WE SHOWED YOU a blueprint for a dream. Well, this is the blueprint, and the dream is Disneyland, the park that we're constructing near Anaheim, California. We promised to keep you informed as our dream became a reality. So, for a firsthand progress report, let's visit Disneyland now. We could go by car, of course—it's a pleasant fifty-minute trip across town. But let's be different. Let's take to the air. Let's go by helicopter."

"DISNEYLAND IS A THING THAT I CAN KEEP MOLDING AND SHAPING. It's a three-dimensional thing to play with. But when I say 'play with it,' I don't mean that. Everything I do I keep a practical eye toward its appeal to the public."

"A LOT OF PEOPLE DON'T REALIZE THAT WE HAVE SOME VERY SERIOUS PROBLEMS HERE, keepin' this thing going and gettin' it started. I remember when we opened, if anybody recalls, we didn't have enough money to finish the landscaping and I had Bill Evans go out and put Latin tags on all the weeds."

"I HAD DIFFERENT COST ESTIMATES; one time it was three and a half million and then I kept fooling around a little more with it and it got up to seven and a half million and I kept fooling around a little more and pretty soon it was twelve and a half and I think when we opened Disneyland it was seventeen million dollars."

"I JUST WANT TO LEAVE YOU WITH THIS THOUGHT, that it's just been a sort of dress rehearsal and that we're just getting started. So if any of you start to rest on your laurels, I mean just forget it, because . . . we are just getting started."

"**DISNEYLAND IS LIKE A PIECE OF CLAY**, if there is something I don't like, I'm not stuck with it. I can reshape and revamp."

"WHENEVER I GO ON A RIDE, I'M ALWAYS THINKING of what's wrong with the thing and how it can be improved."

". . . MORNING COMES AROUND EARLY, and that's one of my favorite times here . . ."

"IT'S NO SECRET THAT WE WERE STICKING JUST ABOUT every nickel we had on the chance that people would really be interested in something totally new and unique in the field of entertainment."

"WE DID IT, IN THE KNOWLEDGE THAT MOST OF THE PEOPLE I talked to thought it would be a financial disaster— closed and forgotten within the first year."

"THE MORE I GO TO OTHER AMUSEMENT PARKS IN ALL PARTS OF THE WORLD, the more I am convinced of the wisdom of the original concepts of Disneyland. I mean, have a single entrance through which all the traffic would flow, then a hub off which the various areas were situated. That gives people a sense of orientation—they know where they are at all times. And it saves a lot of walking."

"DISNEYLAND WILL BE THE ESSENCE OF AMERICA AS WE KNOW IT ... the nostalgia of the past, with exciting glimpses into the future. It will give meaning to the pleasure of the children—and pleasure to the experience of adults ... It will focus a new interest upon Southern California through the mediums of television and other exploitation ... It will be a place for California to be at home, to bring its guests, to demonstrate its faith in the future ... And, mostly, as stated at the beginning—it will be a place for the people to find happiness and knowledge."

"DISNEYLAND IS A SHOW."

"WHEN WE WERE PLANNING DISNEYLAND, we hoped that we could build something that would command the respect of the community and after ten years, I feel that we've accomplished that, not only the community but the country as a whole."

"IT'S SOMETHING THAT WILL NEVER BE FINISHED. Something that I can keep developing, keep plussing and adding to. It's alive. It will be a live breathing thing that will need change. A picture is a thing, once you wrap it up and turn it over to Technicolor, you're through. *Snow White* is a dead issue with me. A live picture I just finished, the one I wrapped up a few weeks ago, it's gone, I can't touch it. There's things in it I don't like; I can't do anything about it. I wanted something alive, something that could grow, something I could keep plussing with ideas; the park is that. Not only can I add things but even the trees will keep growing. The things will get more beautiful each year. And as I find out what the public likes and when a picture's finished and I put it out, I find out what the public doesn't like, I can't change it, it's finished, but I can change the park, because it's alive. That is why I wanted that park."

"I DON'T WANT THE PUBLIC TO SEE THE WORLD they live in while they're in the park. I want them to feel they're in another world."

"DISNEYLAND IS NOT JUST ANOTHER AMUSEMENT PARK. It's unique, and I want it kept that way. Besides, you don't work for a dollar— you work to create and have fun."

"TO MAKE THE DREAM OF DISNEYLAND COME TRUE TOOK the combined skills and talents of hundreds of artisans, carpenters, engineers, scientists and craftsmen. The dream that they built now becomes your heritage. It is you who will make Disneyland truly a magic kingdom and a happy place for the millions of guests who will visit us now and in the future."

"DISNEYLAND IS THE STAR.
Everything else is in the supporting role."

"DISNEYLAND IS OFTEN
CALLED A 'MAGIC KINGDOM'
because it combines fantasy and
history, adventure and learning,
together with every variety of
recreation and fun designed to
appeal to everyone."

ON SNOW AT DISNEYLAND:

"THIS IS VERY UNUSUAL WEATHER FOR SOUTHERN CALIFORNIA—in fact, it's impossible. But since Disneyland is the Magic Kingdom, we thought we'd use some of that magic to create a traditional Christmas atmosphere."

"HERE YOU LEAVE TODAY—
and visit the worlds of yesterday,
tomorrow, and fantasy."

"HERE IS ADVENTURE. HERE
IS ROMANCE. HERE IS MYSTERY.
Tropical rivers—silently flowing
into the unknown. The unbelievable
splendor . . . the eerie sound of the
jungle . . . with eyes that are always
watching. This is Adventureland."

"HERE IS THE WORLD OF
IMAGINATION, HOPES AND DREAMS.
In this timeless land of enchantment, the
age of chivalry, magic and make believe
are reborn—and fairy tales come true.
Fantasyland is dedicated to the young and
the young-in-heart—to those who believe
that when you wish upon a star, your
dreams do come true."

"HERE WE EXPERIENCE THE
STORY OF OUR COUNTRY'S PAST . . .
the colorful drama of Frontier America in
the exciting days of the covered wagon
and the stage coach . . . the advent of the
railroad . . . and the romantic riverboat.
Frontierland is a tribute to the faith,
courage and ingenuity of the pioneers
who blazed the trails across America."

"MAIN STREET, U.S.A. IS AMERICA
AT THE TURN of the century—
the crossroads of an era. The gas lamps
and the electric lamp—the horse-drawn
car and auto car. Main Street is everyone's
hometown—the heartline of America."

"WELL, YOU KNOW THIS DISNEYLAND CONCEPT KEPT GROWING and growing and finally ended up where I felt like I needed two or three hundred acres. So I wanted it in the Southern California area; had certain things that I felt I needed, such as flat land, because I wanted to make my own hills. So I had a survey group go out and hunt for areas that might be useful and they finally came back with several different areas and we settled on Anaheim. The price was right but there was more to it than that, and that is that Anaheim was a sort of a growing area and the freeway project was such that we could see that eventually the freeways would hit Anaheim as a sort of a hub so that's how we selected Anaheim."

"**ANAHEIM WAS A TOWN OF FOURTEEN THOUSAND THEN,** and if someone had mentioned that one year soon six million visitors would come to Disneyland, folks might have had second thoughts about inviting us. In fact, we might have had second thoughts about building a Disneyland!"

"**I FIRST SAW THE SITE FOR DISNEYLAND BACK IN 1953.** In those days, it was all flat land—no rivers, no mountains, no castles or rocket ships— just orange groves, and a few acres of walnut trees."

"Now, when we opened Disneyland, outer space was Buck Rogers. I did put in a trip to the moon. And I got Wernher von Braun to help me plan the thing. And, of course, we were going up to the moon long before Sputnik. And since then has come Sputnik and then has come our great program in outer space. So I had to tear down my Tomorrowland that I built eleven years ago and rebuild it to keep pace."

"It's like the city of tomorrow ought to be. A city that caters to the people as a service function. It will be a planned, controlled community, a showcase for American industry and research, schools, cultural and educational opportunities."

"DISNEYLAND WILL ALWAYS BE BUILDING AND GROWING and adding new things . . . new ways of having fun, of learning things and sharing the many exciting adventures which may be experienced here in the company of family and friends."

"I'VE ALWAYS SAID THERE WILL NEVER BE ANOTHER DISNEYLAND . . .
and I think it's going to work out that way.
But it will be the equivalent of Disneyland.
We know the basic things that have family
appeal. But there's many ways that you
can use those certain basic things and give
them a new decor, a new treatment . . .
this concept here will have to be
something that is unique . . .
so that there is a distinction
between Disneyland in
California and whatever
Disney does
in Florida."

"BUT THE MOST EXCITING AND BY FAR THE MOST IMPORTANT PART of our Florida project—in fact, the heart of everything we'll be doing in Disney World—will be our Experimental Prototype City of Tomorrow! We call it EPCOT . . . spelled E-P-C-O-T . . . Experimental Prototype Community of Tomorrow . . . EPCOT will take its cue from the new ideas and new technologies that are now emerging from the creative centers of American industry. It will be a community of tomorrow that will never be completed, but will always be introducing and testing and demonstrating new materials and systems. And EPCOT will always be a showcase to the world for the ingenuity and imagination of American free enterprise. I don't believe there's a challenge anywhere in the world that's more important to people everywhere than finding solutions to the problems of our cities. But where do we begin—how do we start answering this great challenge? Well, we're convinced we must start with the public need . . ."

"... AND MOST IMPORTANT OF ALL, WHEN EPCOT HAS BECOME a reality and we find the need for technologies that don't even exist today, it's our hope that EPCOT will stimulate American industry to develop new solutions that will meet the needs of people expressed right here in this experimental community."

"WE HAVE DONE A LOT OF THINKING ON A MODEL COMMUNITY, and I would like to be a part of building one, a city of tomorrow, as you might say. I don't believe in going out to this extreme blue sky stuff that some of the architects do. I believe people still want to live like human beings. But there are a lot of things that could be done. I'm not against the automobile but I just feel that you can design so that the automobile is there but still put people back as pedestrians again. I'd love to work on a project like that."

"BUT IF WE CAN BRING TOGETHER THE TECHNICAL know-how of American industry and the creative imagination of the Disney organization—I'm confident we can create right here in Disney World a showcase to the world of the American free enterprise system."

"THE ONE THING I LEARNED FROM DISNEYLAND WAS TO CONTROL THE ENVIRONMENT. Without that we get blamed for the things that someone else does. When they come here they're coming because of an integrity that we've established over the years, and they drive for hundreds of miles and the little hotels on the fringe would jump their rates three times. I've seen it happen and I just can't take it because, I mean, it reflects on us ... I just feel a responsibility to the public when I go into this thing that we must control that ... and when they come into this so-called world, that we will take the blame for what goes on."

"HERE IN FLORIDA, WE HAVE SOMETHING SPECIAL we never enjoyed at Disneyland ... the blessing of size. There's enough land here to hold all the ideas and plans we can possibly imagine."

"BELIEVE ME, IT'S THE MOST EXCITING AND CHALLENGING assignment we have ever tackled at Walt Disney Productions."

"DRAWING UP PLANS AND
DREAMING OF WHAT I COULD DO,
EVERYTHING. It was just something
I kind of kept playing around with."

"DISNEYLAND WILL NEVER BE COMPLETED, as long as there is imagination left in the world."

CHAPTER 5

on business and
The Walt Disney Company

"WITH SOME OF THE BOYS I'D WORKED WITH IN KANSAS CITY AUGMENTING THE SET-UP, I was able to eventually build an organization, and it reached a point that I had so many working with me, and so much time and attention demanded, that I had to drop the drawing end of it myself. But I never regretted it, because drawing was always a means to an end with me."

"THE SECRET OF JUGGLING MANY RESPONSIBILITIES IS ORGANIZATION. Key men are responsible to me and constantly in touch with me to see that I'm there at the right time. These administrators keep things running."

"MY BIG BROTHER ROY WAS ALREADY IN LOS ANGELES as a patient in the Veteran's Hospital. When he got out, we had more in common than brotherly love. Both of us were unemployed and neither could get a job. We solved the problem by going into business for ourselves. We established the first animated cartoon studio in Hollywood."

"**EVERY MAN IS CAPTAIN OF HIS CAREER** and there must be cooperation all around if he is to get what he wants out of life. There is no better time to begin learning this lesson than when we are young, and I think there is no better means of teaching it than through sports programs as well-organized and supervised as Little League baseball. Baseball is a great teacher of an important secret of living: the giving and taking in the group, the development of qualities and behavior that will stand us in good stead through life in pursuits both personal and professional."

"I HAVEN'T DRAWN A SINGLE CHARACTER IN OVER THIRTY YEARS. It's not only that I have no time for it any longer, but I've found development of the stories themselves much more intriguing than drawing. This seems all the more amazing when one considers that each film, no matter how many people have worked on it, has what is called the 'Disney Touch.' The secret is teamwork. Each character is arrived at by group effort. An artist might have a lot of talent and come up with an excellent idea, but if, after it is thoroughly analyzed, the character cannot be adapted and worked with by the group, we discard it."

"RECENTLY SOMEONE POINTED OUT THAT IN THE PAST TEN YEARS we have produced fifty-two feature-length motion pictures, exactly twice the twenty-six features we made in our first three decades, since the day in 1923 when Roy and I went into business making cartoons. Those who have followed our progress know that this figure is typical of what our imaginative staffs have accomplished in recent years, in all areas of our company. The success of *Mary Poppins* and our other films, the worldwide attraction of Disneyland Park, the impact of our color program on network television, and the popularity of our four shows at the New York World's Fair— these things give us confidence that what we do continues to have strong appeal and acceptance by the public."

"WHEN WE CONSIDER A NEW PROJECT, we really study it—not just the surface idea, but everything about it. And when we go into that new project, we believe in it all the way. We have confidence in our ability to do it right. And we work hard to do the best possible job."

"I WANTED TO RETAIN MY INDIVIDUALITY. I was afraid of being hampered by studio policies. I knew if someone else got control, I would be restrained."

"**EVERYONE NEEDS DEADLINES. EVEN THE BEAVERS.** They loaf around all summer, but when they are faced with the winter deadline, they work like fury. If we didn't have deadlines, we'd stagnate."

"**THERE'S REALLY NO SECRET ABOUT OUR APPROACH.** We keep moving forward—opening up new doors and doing new things—because we're curious. And curiosity keeps leading us down new paths. We're always exploring and experimenting. At WED, we call it Imagineering—the blending of creative imagination with technical know-how."

"To keep an operation like Disneyland going, we have to pour it in there … It's what I call 'Keeping the show on the road.' You just have to keep throwing it in. You can't sit back and let it ride. You have to keep throwing it in. Now that's been our policy all our lives. My brother and I have done that, and that is what has built our organization … Not new attractions, but keeping it staffed properly, you know. Never letting your personnel get sloppy, never let them be unfriendly."

"THE FIRST YEAR I LEASED OUT THE PARKING CONCESSION, brought in the usual security guards—things like that. But soon I realized my mistake. I couldn't have outside help and still get over my idea of hospitality. So now we recruit and train every one of our employees. I tell the security police, for instance, that they are never to consider themselves cops. They are there to help people. The visitors are our guests. It's like running a fine restaurant. Once you get the policy going, it grows."

"WELL, I THINK BY THIS TIME MY STAFF, my young group of executives, and everything else, are convinced that Walt is right. That quality will out. And so I think they're going to stay with that policy because it's proved that it's a good business policy. Give the people everything you can give them. Keep the place as clean as you can keep it. Keep it friendly, you know. Make it a real fun place to be. I think they're convinced and I think they'll hang on after, as you say . . . well . . . after Disney."

"THE WAY I SEE IT, DISNEYLAND WILL NEVER BE FINISHED. It's something we can keep developing and adding to. A motion picture is different. Once it's wrapped up and sent out for processing, we're through with it. If there are things that could be improved, we can't do anything about them any more. I've always wanted to work on something alive, something that keeps growing. We've got that in Disneyland."

"GET IN. NOT CHOOSE BUT GET IN. Be part of it and then move up. I've always had that feeling about things. And it upsets me so much when people want to get into something but they're too darn choosy about what they want to do. Get in while you have a chance to at least look and see and out of it might come something."

"A MAN SHOULD NEVER neglect his family for business."

"IF I WERE A FATALIST, OR A MYSTIC, which I decidedly am not, it might be appropriate to say I believe in my lucky star. But I reject 'luck'—I feel every person creates his own 'determinism' by discovering his best aptitudes and following them undeviatingly."

"AS WELL AS I CAN I'M
UNTYING THE APRON STRINGS—
until they scream for help."

"THE INEVITABLE COURSE OF
MOTION PICTURE PRODUCTION has
now brought us to the point where we
must please more people the world
over than ever before, commercially
and artistically. We understand this in
our responsibilities to the trade as well
as for our own welfare in the industry.
Diversity of entertainment therefore
has become our guide and watchword."

"THE WHOLE THING HERE IS THE ORGANIZATION. Whatever we accomplish belongs to our entire group, a tribute to our combined effort. Look at Disneyland. That was started because we had the talents to start it, the talents of the organization. And our World's Fair shows— what we did was possible only because we already had the staff that had worked together for years, blending creative ideas with technical know-how."

"I THINK IF THERE'S ANY PART I'VE PLAYED the vital part is coordinating these talents, and encouraging these talents, and carrying them down a certain line. It's like pulling together a big orchestra. They're all individually very talented. I have an organization of people who are really specialists. You can't match them anywhere in the world for what they can do. But they all need to be pulled together, and that's my job."

"**I'M NOT THE PERFECTIONIST ANYMORE.** It's my staff. They're the ones always insisting on doing something better and better. I'm the fellow trying to hurry them to finish before they spoil the job. You can overwork drawing or writing and lose the spontaneity."

"**No MATTER WHAT THE PROVOCATION,** I never fire a man who is honestly trying to deliver a job. Few workers who become established at the Disney Studio ever leave voluntarily or otherwise, and many have been on the payroll all their working lives."

"OF ALL THE THINGS I'VE DONE, the most vital is coordinating those who work with me and aiming their efforts at a certain goal."

ON WALT DISNEY PRODUCTIONS:

"EVERYTHING HERE IS A TEAM EFFORT."

"WE TRAIN THEM TO BE AWARE that they're there mainly to help the guests."

"ANYTHING THAT HAS A DISNEY NAME TO IT is something we feel responsible for."

"MY ROLE? WELL, YOU KNOW I WAS STUMPED ONE DAY WHEN A LITTLE BOY ASKED, 'Do you draw Mickey Mouse?' I had to admit I do not draw anymore. 'Then you think up all the jokes and ideas?' 'No,' I said, 'I don't do that.' Finally, he looked at me and said, 'Mr. Disney, just what do you do?' 'Well,' I said, 'sometimes I think of myself as a little bee. I go from one area of the studio to another and gather pollen and sort of stimulate everybody. I guess that's the job I do.'"

"I DON'T POSE AS AN AUTHORITY ON ANYTHING AT ALL, I follow the opinions of the ordinary people I meet, and I take pride in the close-knit teamwork with my organization."

"MOST OF MY LIFE I HAVE DONE WHAT I WANTED TO DO. I have had fun on the job. I have never been able to confine that fun to office hours."

"Whatever we accomplish
is due to the combined effort.
The organization must be with you or
you don't get it done; they just say to
heck with him, let him do it himself.
In my organization there is respect for
every individual, and we all have a keen
respect for the public."

CHAPTER 6

on success and failure

"**THERE'S A GREAT FEELING OF SATISFACTION IN WINNING AN AWARD FOR A JOB WELL DONE,** whether it be for winning a foot race, designing a rocket or making a motion picture. Now, we haven't done too well with the first two on the list, but pictures, that's something else. No one person can take credit for the success of a motion picture. It's strictly a team effort. From the time the story is written to the time the final release print comes off the printer, hundreds of people are involved— each one doing a job—each job contributing to the final product. And—if the picture wins an award, the feeling of satisfaction we were speaking of can rightfully be shared by each and every one."

"I HAVE BEEN UP AGAINST TOUGH COMPETITION ALL MY LIFE. I wouldn't know how to get along without it."

"ALMOST EVERYONE WARNED US THAT DISNEYLAND WOULD BE A HOLLYWOOD SPECTACULAR—a spectacular failure. But they were thinking about an amusement park, and we believed in our idea—a family park where parents and children could have fun—together."

"ALL THE ADVERSITY I'VE HAD IN MY LIFE, all my troubles and obstacles have strengthened me."

"YOU MAY NOT REALIZE IT WHEN IT HAPPENS, but a kick in the teeth may be the best thing in the world for you."

"I THINK IT'S IMPORTANT TO HAVE
A GOOD HARD FAILURE WHEN
YOU'RE YOUNG. I learned a lot out
of that. Because it makes you kind
of aware of what can happen to you.
Because of it I've never had any fear
in my whole life when we've been
near collapse and all of that. I've
never been afraid. I've never had the
feeling I couldn't walk out and get
a job doing something."

"IT IS GOOD TO HAVE A FAILURE WHILE YOU'RE YOUNG because it teaches you so much. For one thing it makes you aware that such a thing can happen to anybody, and once you've lived through the worst, you're never quite as vulnerable afterward."

"GET A GOOD IDEA, AND STAY WITH IT. Dog it, and work at it until it's done, and done right."

"To some people, I am kind of a Merlin who takes lots of crazy chances, but rarely makes mistakes. I've made some bad ones, but fortunately, the successes have come along fast enough to cover up the mistakes. When you go to bat as many times as I do, you're bound to get a good average. That's why I keep my projects diversified."

"NATURALLY WE ARE ALL EXTREMELY GRATIFIED by the reception given *Snow White*, for it shows us conclusively that the public is ready for more animated features."

"PEOPLE OFTEN ASK ME IF I KNOW THE SECRET OF SUCCESS and if I could tell others how to make their dreams come true. My answer is you do it by working."

"I'D LIKE TO ADD ONE THOUGHT TO THE SUBJECT OF SUCCESS and the claims made for it as a deserved reward for effort and understanding. It seems to me shallow and arrogant for any man in these times to claim he is completely self-made, that he owes all his success to his own unaided efforts. While, of course, it is basic Americanism that a man's standing is in part due to his personal enterprise and capacity, it is equally true that many hands and hearts and minds generally contribute to anyone's notable achievements. We share, to a large extent, one another's fate. We help create those circumstances which favor or challenge us in meeting our objectives and realizing our dreams. There is great comfort and inspiration in this feeling of close human relationships and its bearing on our mutual fortunes—a powerful force to overcome the 'tough breaks' which are certain to come to most of us from time to time."

"WE GREW TO OUR PRESENT SIZE ALMOST AGAINST OURSELVES. It was not a deliberately planned commercial venture in the sense that I sat down and said that we were going to make ourselves into a huge financial octopus. We evolved by necessity. We did not sit down and say to ourselves, 'How can we make a big pile of dough?' It just happened."

"I FUNCTION BETTER WHEN THINGS ARE GOING BADLY than when they're as smooth as whipped cream."

"I SUPPOSE MY FORMULA MIGHT BE: dream, diversify—and never miss an angle."

CHAPTER 7

on money

"MONEY ISN'T EVERYTHING. . . .
IT MAY NOT ACTUALLY BE the
root of all evil but it can't buy peace,
contentment or happiness, you know."

"CARTOON FEATURES GIVE US OUR BIGGEST FINANCIAL PROBLEMS. They take a lot of manpower that could produce much more in other fields. Like most luxuries, however, there is solid value in the feature cartoon. While they're expensive, they are also prestige builders."

"THE IDEA FOR DISNEYLAND LAY DORMANT FOR SEVERAL YEARS. It came along when I was taking my kids around to these kiddie parks ... and while they were on the merry-go-round riding forty times or something, I'd be sitting there trying to figure what I could do. When I built the studio I thought we ought to have a three-dimension thing that people could actually come and visit—they can't visit our studio, because the rooms are small. So I had a little dream for Disneyland adjoining the studio, but I couldn't get anybody to go in with me because we were going through this depression. And whenever I'd go down and talk to my brother about it, why he'd always suddenly get busy with some figures so, I mean, I didn't dare bring it up. But I kept working on it and I worked on it with my own money. Not the studio's money, but my own money."

"EVERYBODY THINKS THAT THE PARK IS A GOLD MINE—but we have had our problems. You've got to work it and know how to handle it. Even trying to keep that park clean is a tremendous expense. And those sharp pencil guys tell you, 'Walt, if we cut down on maintenance, we'd save a lot of money.' But I don't believe in that—it's like any other show on the road; it must be kept clean and fresh."

"I COULD NEVER CONVINCE THE FINANCIERS THAT DISNEYLAND WAS FEASIBLE, because dreams offer too little collateral."

"I AM NOT AN ECONOMIST, BUT THINGS ARE NOT AS BAD AS THEY SEEM. I have a great deal of confidence in our future."

"HAPPINESS IS A STATE OF MIND . . . It's just according to the way you look at things. So I think happiness is contentment but it doesn't mean you have to have wealth. All individuals are different and some of us just wouldn't be satisfied with just carrying out a routine job and being happy."

"YOU REACH A POINT WHERE you don't work for money."

"MONEY IS SOMETHING I UNDERSTAND ONLY VAGUELY, and think about it only when I don't have enough to finance my current enthusiasm, whatever it may be. All I know about money is that I have to have it to do things. I don't want to bank my dividends, I'd rather keep my money working. I regard it as a moral obligation to pay back borrowed money. When I make a profit, I don't squander it or hide it away; I immediately plow it back into a fresh project. I have little respect for money as such; I regard it merely as a medium for financing new ideas. I neither wish nor intend to amass a personal fortune. Money—or, rather the lack of it to carry out my ideas—may worry me, but it does not excite me. Ideas excite me."

"BIGGEST PROBLEM? WELL, I'D SAY IT'S BEEN MY BIGGEST PROBLEM ALL MY LIFE. Money. It takes a lot of money to make these dreams come true. From the very start it was a problem. Getting the money to open Disneyland. About seventeen million it took. And we had everything mortgaged including my family. But we were able to get it open and in the ten or eleven years now we have been pouring more money back in. In other words, like the old farmer, you have got to pour it back in the ground if you want it to grow. That's my brother's philosophy and mine, too."

"I'VE ALWAYS BEEN BORED WITH JUST MAKING MONEY. I've wanted to do things; I wanted to build things, to get something going. What money meant to me was that I was able to get money to do that for me."

"RECESSION DOESN'T DESERVE THE RIGHT TO EXIST. There are just too many things to be done in science and engineering to be bogged down by temporary economic dislocations."

"SOME PEOPLE FORGET THAT YOU CAN STILL DO GOOD WORK EVEN THOUGH you work with dollar bills. We took almost nine years to make *Fantasia*, and if we had to do it again I'd take a long hard look at it, because today it would cost us fifteen million. At some stage or other I have to walk in and tell the boys: 'O.K. Start wrapping it up.' If I didn't, we'd never get the work finished. But that doesn't mean we pull back on quality."

"**I ACTUALLY STARTED TO PLAN THE PICTURE ABOUT 1935.** And I fooled around with it, trying to get a hold of a story and things, for a couple of years, and finally it began to jell, then I went to work on it and I finished in the fall of 1937. I didn't know what I had or what would happen or anything. We had the family fortune, we had everything wrapped up in *Snow White*. In fact the bankers, I think, were losing more sleep than I was. And fortunately, though, when we put it in and premiered it and everything else, why everything was fine and the bankers were happy."

"WHEN SNOW WHITE HIT, WE REALIZED WE WERE IN A NEW BUSINESS. We knew it within a week after the picture had opened at the Carthay Circle in Los Angeles. We had been heavily in debt and within six months we had millions in the bank."

CHAPTER 8

on children, young and old

"YOU KNOW . . . THERE'S ONE THING I KNOW ABOUT KIDS—just when you figure you've got them figured they come up with something you never figured on. That's what makes them interesting. And I wouldn't change them for the world."

"ADULTS ARE INTERESTED IF YOU DON'T PLAY DOWN to the little two or three year olds or talk down. I don't believe in talking down to children. I don't believe in talking down to any certain segment. I like to kind of just talk in a general way to the audience. Children are always reaching."

"DESPITE ALL THE PUBLICITY ABOUT DELINQUENCY, America's youngsters are a pretty good lot. One of the things I want to do is make a picture that shows the good side of teenagers. I get so put out with all these pictures about delinquency. One picture upset me for three days afterward. I think these pictures are a mistake. Children get bad ideas when they see such things on the screen. And I don't think they show a true picture of young people today."

"OVER AT OUR PLACE, WE'RE
SURE OF JUST ONE THING:
everybody in the world was once a
child ... So, when planning a new
picture, we don't think of grownups
and we don't think of children, but just
of that fine, clean, unspoiled spot, down
deep in every one of us that maybe
the world has made us forget, and that
maybe our pictures can help recall."

"I DO NOT MAKE FILMS PRIMARILY FOR CHILDREN. I make them for the child in all of us, whether we be six or sixty. Call the child innocence. The worst of us is not without innocence, although buried deeply it might be. In my work I try to reach and speak to that innocence, showing it the fun and joy of living; showing it that laughter is healthy; showing it that the human species, although happily ridiculous at times, is still reaching for the stars."

"A CHILD IS HELPLESS IN CHOOSING WHAT IS TO BE ENGRAVEN ON HIS MIND during the formative years. The awesome responsibility is assumed, for better or worse, by us adults. Today we are shapers of the world of tomorrow. That is the plain truth. There is no way we can duck the responsibility; and there is no reason, except sloth and cowardice, why we should."

"**I DIDN'T TREAT MY YOUNGSTERS LIKE FRAIL FLOWERS,** and I think no parent should. Children are people, and they should have to reach to learn about things, to understand things, just as adults have to reach if they want to grow in mental stature. Life is composed of lights and shadows, and we would be untruthful, insincere and saccharine if we tried to pretend there were no shadows. Most things are good, and they are the strongest things, but there are evil things, too, and you could do a child no favor by trying to shield it from reality. The important thing is to teach a child that good can always triumph over evil, and that is what our pictures do."

"EVERY CHILD IS BORN BLESSED WITH A VIVID IMAGINATION. But just as a muscle grows flabby with disuse so the bright imagination of a child pales in later years if he ceases to exercise it."

"WHY DO WE HAVE TO GROW UP? I know more adults who have the children's approach to life. They're people who don't give a hang what the Joneses do. You see them at Disneyland every time you go there. They are not afraid to be delighted with simple pleasures, and they have a degree of contentment with what life has brought—sometimes it isn't much, either."

"I THINK OF A NEWBORN BABY'S MIND AS A BLANK BOOK. During the first years of his life much will be written on the pages. The quality of the writing, whatever it be, will affect his life profoundly. Let us multiply that single mind by millions. What is written on that enormity of youthful minds will alter the course of the world. This is how history is determined. It is self-evident to anybody who studies the history of human races."

"I HAVE NEVER MADE PICTURES EXCLUSIVELY FOR CHILDREN. But I regard them as important members of the family, and we have always considered their age, experience, and taste in selecting our theatrical productions."

"MOVIES CAN AND DO HAVE TREMENDOUS INFLUENCE IN SHAPING YOUNG LIVES in the realm of entertainment toward the ideals and objectives of normal adulthood."

"MY BUSINESS IS MAKING PEOPLE, ESPECIALLY CHILDREN, HAPPY. I have dedicated much of my time to a study of the problems of children."

"CHILDREN ARE MORE INTELLIGENT TODAY because their experience is greater. Exposure and schools are better. They have access to visual education in the schools. The imagination of the teacher is supplemented by the best visual aids. She in turn is stimulated and gets as much out of the films as the student does."

"THE AMERICAN CHILD IS A HIGHLY INTELLIGENT HUMAN BEING—characteristically sensitive, humorous, open-minded, eager to learn, and has a strong sense of excitement, energy and healthy curiosity about the world in which he lives. Lucky indeed is the grownup who manages to carry these same characteristics over into his adult life. It usually makes for a happy and successful individual."

"You're Dead If You Aim Only For Kids. Adults are only kids grown up, anyway."

"I DO NOT MAKE PICTURES FOR CHILDREN, at least not just for children. I won't play down to them. Too many people grow up. That's the real trouble with the world, too many people grow up. They forget. They don't remember what it's like to be twelve years old. They patronize; they treat children as inferiors. I won't do that. I'll temper a story, yes. But I won't play down, and I won't patronize."

"ESSENTIALLY, THE REAL DIFFERENCE BETWEEN A CHILD AND AN ADULT IS EXPERIENCE. We conceive it to be our job on the *Mickey Mouse Club* show to provide some of that experience. Happy, factual, constructive experience whenever possible."

ABOUT DISNEYLAND:

"IT HAS THAT THING— THE IMAGINATION, and the feeling of happy excitement— I knew when I was a kid."

"IN THE WINTERTIME YOU CAN GO OUT THERE during the week and you won't see any children. You'll see the oldsters out there riding all these rides and having fun and everything. Summertime, of course, the average would drop down. But the overall, year-round average, it's four adults to one child."

"I THINK WE HAVE MADE
THE FAIRY TALE FASHIONABLE AGAIN.
That is, our own blend of theatrical
mythology. The fairy tale of film—created
with the magic of animation—is the
modern equivalent of the great parables of
the Middle Ages. Creation is the word. Not
adaptation. Not version. We can translate
the ancient fairy tale into its modern
equivalent without losing the lovely patina
and the savor of its once-upon-a-time
quality. I think our films have
brought new adult respect
for the fairy tale. We have
proved that the age-old
kind of entertainment
based on the classic
fairy tale recognizes no
young, no old."

"PART OF THE DISNEY SUCCESS IS OUR ABILITY TO CREATE a believable world of dreams that appeals to all age groups. The kind of entertainment we create is meant to appeal to every member of the family."

"IT'S A MISTAKE NOT TO GIVE PEOPLE A CHANCE to learn to depend on themselves while they are young."

"PEOPLE SORT OF LIVE IN THE DARK ABOUT THINGS. A lot of young people think the future is closed to them, that everything has been done. This is not so. There are still plenty of avenues to be explored."

"YOU CAN'T LIVE ON THINGS MADE FOR CHILDREN—OR FOR CRITICS. I've never made films for either of them. Disneyland is not just for children. I don't play down."

"BUT NOW, LOOKING BACK, I HAVE SATISFACTION, even pleasure, in tracing the effects these newspaper-delivery days had on my mature life. Now I can appreciate the self-reliance, self-discipline, and self-wisdom gained from those responsibilities. . . . The sense of responsibility— yes, this I believe is the most valuable thing a boy can carry along into later life from his first job."

"CHILDISHNESS? I THINK IT'S THE EQUIVALENT OF never losing your sense of humor. I mean, there's a certain something that you retain. It's the equivalent of not getting so stuffy that you can't laugh at others."

"TO THE YOUNGSTERS OF TODAY, I say believe in the future, the world is getting better; there still is plenty of opportunity. Why, would you believe it, when I was a kid I thought it was already too late for me to make good at anything."

CHAPTER 9

on family

"THE IMPORTANT THING IS THE FAMILY. If you can keep the family together—and that's the backbone of our whole business, catering to families—that's what we hope to do."

"THE MOST IMPORTANT THING BROUGHT ABOUT in the past quarter century of motion-picture history is the recognition that amusement, recreation, mass diversion, is no longer a dispensable luxury. Family fun is as necessary to modern living as a kitchen refrigerator."

"PEOPLE ARE ALWAYS ANALYZING OUR APPROACH TO ENTERTAINMENT. Some reporters have called it the 'special secret' of Disney entertainment. Well, we like a little mystery in our films, but there's really no secret about our approach. We're not out to make a fast dollar with gimmicks. We're interested in doing things that are fun—in bringing pleasure and especially laughter to people. And we have never lost our faith in *family* entertainment stories that make people laugh, stories about warm and human things, stories about historic characters and events, and stories about animals."

"**WE THINK OF THE FAMILY AUDIENCE.** Mickey Mouse would not have been the success he was were it not for the broad appeal. We are not playing just for kids. If you took your kids to the movies and left them there to be picked up later and did not go in yourself, I'd feel unhappy. After all, if you are aiming at the kids, what age would you aim at?"

"**WE TRY IT IN EVERYTHING WE DO HERE,** you know for the family. We don't actually make films for children. But we make films that children can enjoy along with their parents."

"A FAMILY PICTURE IS ONE THE KIDS CAN TAKE THEIR PARENTS TO see and not be embarrassed. I think that by producing family films we reach the audience which has been dormant at the box office for a long time. I don't like downbeat pictures and I cannot believe that the average family does either. Personally, when I go to the theater I don't want to come out depressed. That's why we make the kind of films so many label 'Family Type.' We avoid messages and have opened up new doors and broadened the field for ourselves by producing human stories, with comedy and drama mixed."

CHAPTER 10

on education

"YOU'LL BE A POORER PERSON ALL YOUR LIFE if you don't know some of the great stories and the great poems. But the actual world of nature and human nature is where you will live and work with your neighbors and your competitors. So keep your eyes open."

"IT HAS ALWAYS BEEN MY HOPE THAT OUR fairy tale films will result in a desire of viewers to read again the fine old original tales and enchanting myths on the home bookshelf or school library. Our motion picture productions are designed to augment them, not to supplant them."

"CROWDED CLASSROOMS AND HALF-DAY SESSIONS are a tragic waste of our greatest national resource— the minds of our children."

"No one can have a well-rounded education without some knowledge of what goes on in the physical world around us. He must have some orderly information about the earth and its multitude of animal wayfarers. They have helped define our culture, our arts, our behaviorism, and, indeed, the fundamentals of our human civilization."

"THE THEATER OF EDUCATION
WILL BE ANY MARKETPLACE,
public square, hill or dale where power
can be found to project a motion
picture on a screen."

"WE HAVE LONG HELD THAT
THE NORMAL GAP between
what is generally regarded as
'entertainment' and what is defined
'educational' represents an old and
untenable viewpoint."

"THE AGE WE'RE LIVING IN IS THE MOST EXTRAORDINARY the world has ever seen. There are whole new concepts of things, and we now have the tools to change these concepts into realities. We're moving forward. In terms of my work, I believe people want to know about this universe that keeps unfolding before them. But let's be clear about one thing—I'm not trying to teach anything to anybody. I want to entertain the public."

"THE FIRST THING I DID WHEN I GOT A LITTLE MONEY TO EXPERIMENT, I put all my artists back in school. The art school that existed then didn't quite have enough for what we needed, so we set up our own art school."

"PICTURE AUDIENCES WANT TO KNOW THINGS rather than escape realities, so long as they are presented as entertainment. There now is such passion for learning as has never before swept this country and the world."

"SCHOOL-AGE YOUNGSTERS ARE CAPABLE OF ABSORBING and retaining a tremendous amount of learning. Given the chance, they have an amazing aptitude for knowledge. We must not deny them that chance through shortages of classrooms and inadequate educational facilities. Having spent most of my life creating material for children and observing their potential, I feel convinced that a full-time education for our youth is our best investment in the future."

"I AM NOT TRYING TO BE A TEACHER. I want to make stories to apply to a broad field so that mother and father can understand the need and will help the child. If we can accomplish that, our work has been worthwhile."

"THE ASSURANCE TO ACADEMIC LEADERS THAT 'WE ALSO TEACH' in the expanding scheme of public education will continue to be an inspiration to all of us who share as a team in the production of pictures which are intended to, at once, delight the senses and to appeal to the mind."

"WE HAVE ALWAYS TRIED TO BE GUIDED BY THE BASIC IDEA THAT, in the discovery of knowledge, there is great entertainment—as, conversely, in all good entertainment there is always some grain of wisdom, humanity or enlightenment to be gained."

"THE FUTURE OF THE ANIMATED EDUCATIONAL movie seems as limitless as the variety of things we can portray in it."

"HUMANS LEARNED LIFE'S LESSONS BY SEEING REAL THINGS or pictures with their eyes for ages before they began learning through written or spoken words, so it is not strange that they still learn most readily by pictures. The animated cartoon can set forth anything from a world in evolution to the whirl of electrons invisible to human eyes; can produce a mosquito tall enough to tower over a village or a fairy small enough to dance on a leaf; can get inside a complex machine, slow down its action, explain its operation to apprentices with a clarity impossible in any other medium, and can even get inside the human body."

"WE LEARNED A GREAT
DEAL DURING THE war years when
we were making instruction and
technological films in which abstract
and obscure things had to be made
plain and quickly and exactly applicable
to the men in the military services.
These explorations and efficiencies
of our cartoon medium must not be
unused in the entertainment field."

"EDUCATIONAL FILMS WILL NEVER REPLACE THE TEACHER. The three R's are basic (reading, 'riting, 'rithmetic), but their advancement by means of the motion picture screen will give more people in this world an opportunity to learn. Pictures can make both teaching and learning a pleasure. And educators agree that when a student has begun to learn and like it, half their problem is solved."

"RECENTLY OUR ANIMATION TECHNIQUES HAVE been applied to scientific subjects, accomplishing the feat of translating the abstractions of biology, chemistry, astronomy and space engineering into popularly understood terms of theatrical entertainment."

"I DO NOT WANT TO MAKE TEACHING FILMS. If I did, I would create a separate organization. It is not higher education that interests me so much as general mass education."

"THE CARTOON IS A GOOD MEDIUM TO STIMULATE INTEREST. It is an ideal medium for teaching and it has always been my hope that we could do something that way. But it would have to be of general interest, yet helpful in teaching. It should be used for opening people's minds and meeting their needs. We have recently explained mathematics in a film and in that way excited public interest in this very important subject. *Donald in Mathmagic Land* stimulated interest in mathematics and turned out very well."

"THE POSSIBILITIES OF THE ANIMATED CARTOON as a medium of education is virtually limitless. Its field is bound only by the capability of men to use it for its full possibilities."

"WHEN THE SUBJECT PERMITS, WE LET FLY with all the satire and gags at our command. Laughter is no enemy to learning."

"... THE MEDIUM OF THE ANIMATED FILM is perhaps the most flexible, versatile and stimulating of all teaching facilities. The question now is where, how and with what means the educational film shall be included in the tool kit of the pedagogue."

"EQUALLY IMPORTANT AND ABSORBING, both as information and as sheer entertainment, will be our ventures into the world of the invisible and the inaudible: Things like the processes going on in a man's body, or the functioning of his mind."

"IN CONSIDERING OUR FILMS FROM A FORMAL EDUCATIONAL viewpoint and as an example of technical practice, the factual nature picture presents unique possibilities. Nature herself offers as exciting documents her own living creatures. They are not obscure abstractions."

"I'VE ALWAYS HAD THE FEELING AND I've always felt that there's a thing that schools should put more emphasis on . . . that is how to research. I think it is what more students should know. Take even a lawyer who's spent years in school. Where would he be without his library? I see writers who're supposed to be well-educated and everything else. You go in where they're working, you see all the different books they have around and everything else and the dictionaries they have there, the tools of their trade."

CHAPTER 11

on America

"OUR HERITAGE AND IDEALS,
OUR CODE AND STANDARDS, the
things we live by and teach our children
are preserved or diminished by how
freely we exchange ideas and feelings."

"PHYSICAL AMERICA—THE LAND ITSELF—should be as dear to us all as our political heritage and our treasured way of life. Its preservation and the wise conservation of its renewable resources concerns every man, woman, and child whose possession it is."

"RECENTLY I WAS INVITED TO SEE A SHOW ON AMERICA, and as I sat there watching and listening I felt both proud and thrilled; thrilled with the voices, thrilled with the sounds; proud of the group of one hundred talented young Americans singing about our country. The songs that made me proud of being an American."

"**EVERYONE LOVES A CIRCUS, AND I'M NO EXCEPTION.** I've been fascinated by the clowns and the animals, the music and the excitement ever since I worked in one of these wonderful shows for a few days as a youngster."

"**YES-SIRREE, SEE THE WORLD FROM THE BIG TOP—GLAMOUR**—excitement— win fame and fortune—all that sort of thing. Well, it was mighty nice to dream about, but I don't believe many boys ever actually got around to doing it. I know I didn't."

"AMERICANS ARE A RESPONSIVE PEOPLE AND THE IDEAS, the knowledge and the emotions that come through the television screen in our living rooms will most certainly shape the course of the future for ourselves and our children."

"ACTUALLY, IF YOU COULD SEE CLOSE IN MY EYES, the American flag is waving in both of them and up my spine is growing this red, white and blue stripe."

"I GET RED, WHITE AND
BLUE AT TIMES."

"I'VE ALWAYS BEEN A
KIND OF A BILLBOARD
AMERICAN. I think I get that
red, white and blue streak up
and down my back every once
in a while."

CHAPTER 12

on animals and nature

"FABLE ANIMALS ARE NOT REAL ANIMALS. They are human beings in the guise of bird and beast. From his earliest beginnings, as his cave drawings eloquently attest, man has been telling many of his experiences and dramatic conclusions and comments through animal symbols."

"WHAT I HAVE LEARNED FROM THE ANIMAL WORLD, and what anyone will learn who studies it, is a renewed sense of kinship with the earth and all its inhabitants."

"NEXT TO HIS OWN MOST INTIMATE SELF-CONCERNS, man is most fascinated by creatures of the animal kingdom. They have been close to his interest and his fate from time beyond the Ark."

"WHY DO ANIMALS DOMINATE ANIMATED CARTOONS? Because

their reaction to any kind of stimulus is expressed physically. Often the entire body comes into play. Take a joyful dog. His tail wags, his torso wiggles, his ears flap. He may greet you by jumping on your lap or by making the circuit of the room, not missing a chair or a divan. He keeps barking, and that's a form of physical expression, too; he stretches his big mouth. But how does a human being react to a stimulus? He's lost the sense of play he once had and he inhibits physical expression. He is the victim of a civilization whose ideal is the unbotherable, poker-faced man and the attractive, unruffled woman. Even the gestures get to be calculated. They call it poise. The spontaneity of the animal, you find it in small children, but it's gradually trained out of them."

"ANIMALS HAVE PERSONALITIES like people and must be studied."

"MANY PEOPLE REGARD THE ELEPHANT AS A SYMBOL OF GOOD LUCK. We at the studio sort of share that view."

"ALL CARTOON ANIMALS MUST BE JUDGED by their story intent and relationship as a matter of basic procedure in creating animation entertainment. Cartoon animals, of course, are not and never were replicas of real animals; they are a special breed of creatures out of the world of fable who duplicate human traits and foibles rather than those of the real animal kingdom. Mickey Mouse was never a mouse nor anything like a mouse; no more was Donald ever a duck."

"WE CAN LEARN A LOT FROM NATURE IN ACTION. Among other things, this: Each creature must earn his right to live and survive by his own efforts, according to his wit and energy and the things which in human relations we call moral behavior."

"I DON'T LIKE FORMAL GARDENS. I like wild nature. It's just the wilderness instinct in me, I guess."

"DESPITE THEIR COUNTLESS
NUMBERS, few people ever
glimpse more than the commonest
breed of birds and beast. Nature—if
we may speak of her as a universal
intelligence—jealously guards her
secret activities."

"THE IMMEDIATE NEED FOR EDUCATION AND practice in using our natural resources of soil, forest, water, wildlife and areas of inspirational beauty to the best advantage of all, for this generation and others to come, is again apparent to every observant citizen. My interest in these problems has been sharpened by our motion picture production of wildlife subjects and the relation of animal life to all the other conservation issues during the past few years."

"IF CERTAIN EVENTS CONTINUE, much of America's natural beauty will become nothing more than a memory. The natural beauty of America is a treasure found nowhere else in the world. Our forests, waters, grasslands, and wildlife must be wisely protected and used. I urge all citizens to join the effort to save America's natural beauty . . . it's our America—do something to preserve its beauty, strength, and natural wealth."

"WHEN I FIRST SAW
MINERAL KING, I thought it
was one of the most beautiful places
in the world, and we want to keep
it that way. With its development
we will prove once again that man
and nature can work together to the
benefit of both."

"IT IS OUR PLAN TO MAKE MINERAL KING a year-round outdoor recreational adventure for everyone ... a challenge to the accomplished skier and a good place to put skis on for the first time ... the ideal spot for an old-fashioned family outing ... home base for wild-life students, hikers, fishermen and campers ... the perfect retreat for those who just want to get away for a breath of fresh, invigorating mountain air."

"OUR WHOLE MASTER PLAN FOR THIS REGION is based on two very important needs. First is the necessity to preserve the great natural beauty of the site. That is a must. Second, we want Mineral King to become a year-round recreational facility for everyone, regardless of age or athletic abilities."

"TO ALL OF US, THE DEVELOPMENT of Mineral King represents both a challenge and an obligation; a challenge to create, design and operate facilities that serve the ever-growing public need and the interest of participants. It is also an obligation to preserve nature's gifts to Mineral King."

"WHEN WE GO INTO A NEW PROJECT, we believe in it all the way. That's the way we feel about Mineral King. We have every faith that our plans will provide recreational opportunities for everyone. All of us promise that our efforts now and in the future will be dedicated to making Mineral King grow to meet the ever-increasing public need. I guess you might say that it won't ever be finished."

"WE BELIEVE THAT MINERAL KING SHOULD BE much more than the best place to spend a vacation or holiday. We want it to be an experience with the outdoors for those who love nature—or who want to learn to love it."

"WE DID NOT SUCCUMB TO THE ALLURING TEMPTATIONS to make villains or saints of the creatures portrayed in our films. We have maintained a sensitive regard for the wisdom of Nature's design and have attempted to hold a mirror to the out-of-doors rather than to interpret its functioning by man's standards. Our films have provided thrilling entertainment of educational quality and have played a major part in the worldwide increase in appreciation and understanding of nature. These films have demonstrated that facts can be as fascinating as fiction, truth as beguiling as myth, and have opened the eyes of young and old to the beauties of the outdoor world and aroused their desire to conserve priceless natural assets."

CHAPTER 13

on art, music, and dance

"I DON'T PRETEND TO KNOW ANYTHING ABOUT ART. I make pictures for entertainment, and then the professors tell me what they mean."

"I'VE NEVER CALLED MY WORK AN 'ART.' It's part of show business, the business of building entertainment."

"I AM IN NO SENSE OF THE WORD A GREAT ARTIST, not even a great animator; I have always had men working for me whose skills were greater than my own. I am an idea man."

"I LIKE SYMPHONIC MUSIC. A GOOD CONCERT, if you're kind of relaxed, it can do something to you. It's sort of an emotional break you get by listening to the music."

225

"MUSIC HAS ALWAYS HAD A PROMINENT PART IN ALL OUR PRODUCTS, from the early cartoon days. So much so, in fact, that I cannot think of the pictorial story without thinking about the complementary music which will fulfill it. Often the musical theme comes first, suggesting a way of treatment. This was the case with the Tchaikovsky music for *Sleeping Beauty* which finally formulated our presentation of the classic. I have had no formal musical training. But by long experience and by strong personal leaning, the selection of musical themes, original or adapted, we were guided to wide audience acceptance. Credit for the memorable songs and scores must, of course, go to the brilliant composers and musicians who have been associated with me through the years."

"POSSIBLY THE *THREE LITTLE PIGS* CAME OUT at just the right psychological moment—in 1933 a lot of people were talking about keeping the wolf from the door. At any rate, both the picture and song were quite successful—and important to us in another way as well. They showed us the value of telling a story through a song. When we started *Snow White*, the first feature length cartoon, we kept this in mind. Of course, we wanted the songs to stand on their own merits . . . and most of them did very well. But our first concern was to make sure that each song helped us tell our story."

"THROUGHOUT OUR CAREER IN MOTION PICTURES, classical music has played a very important part. Early in the beginning we created a cartoon series called Silly Symphonies . . . simple short subjects that relied heavily on the works of classical composers. The popularity of the Silly Symphonies led us to undertake a major effort, *Fantasia*, which featured the music of Bach, Dukas, Tchaikovsky, Stravinsky, Moussorgsky, Beethoven and Schubert."

ON *SNOW WHITE AND THE SEVEN DWARFS*:

"IT'S NO MORE A CARTOON than a painting by Whistler is a cartoon."

"You know, I never miss dropping in at the Plaza Gardens. Like most people, I have fun watching others have fun. . . . I get tired just watching the kids dance . . . oh, to be thirty years younger."

"In 1940, we decided to animate a satire of the famous ballet, 'The Dance of the Hours,' for our musical feature *Fantasia*. While ballet has inspired many beautiful works of art like this painting by Degas . . . it had scarcely been touched upon in the field of animation. In fact, our animators knew very little about it, and because a thorough knowledge of a subject is essential in order to caricature it . . . a new course was added to our studio school curriculum . . . Classical Ballet."

CHAPTER 14

on progress and innovation

"**IT'S A SORT OF ANOTHER DOOR THAT'S OPENED FOR US.** You see our whole forty-some-odd-years here has been in the world of making things move—inanimate things move. From a drawing board through all kinds of any little props and things. Now we're making these human figures, dimensional human figures move, making animals move, making anything move through the use of electronics. It's a tape mechanism, it's like programming or sequencing when they're sending missiles to the moon."

"I FIGURED IT WOULD TAKE ME TEN YEARS TO GET MR. LINCOLN GOING.

Well, I had him in what we called *Mark I* and I had him under manual control. We could make him stand up and put his hand out. Robert Moses was getting the World's Fair going, and he came out. He came and visited Disneyland. He wanted to visit the studio. He was trying to get ideas on what could be done. So I had him meet Abraham Lincoln. I said, 'Would you like to meet Mr. Lincoln?' He gave me a funny look. I said, 'Well, come on in—meet him.' So when he walked in the door, I said, 'Mr. Lincoln, meet Mr. Moses,' and Lincoln stood up and put his hand out and Moses went over and shook hands with him. Well, Moses is quite a showman, and he said, 'I've got to have Lincoln in the Fair.' But I said, 'This is five years away, anyway.' But Moses wouldn't take no for an answer. The next thing I knew he had gotten with the State of Illinois and was trying to sell them on a pavilion. And before I knew it, I had my arm twisted and I said yes. We now had to get Mr. Lincoln on the road, I think, in about thirteen months."

"IT'S SOUND AND ANIMATION THROUGH ELECTRONICS. It's opened a whole new door for us. We can program whole shows on a tape. The tape sends signals, and the little figures go to work and they sing and act and move according to the impulse that comes from the tape. And this is all possible because of this big drive that we've had on the space age development, the electronic age."

"MANY OF THESE ATTRACTIONS WILL 'COME TO LIFE' through Audio-Animatronics, our space-age electronic method of making inanimate things move on cue, hour after hour and show after show."

"OF ALL OUR INVENTIONS FOR MASS COMMUNICATION, pictures still speak the most universally understood language."

"IT IS TO THE NATURE OF OUR COMMUNICATIONS that we must look for the benefactions which can come from such interchange. The machinery stands ready, is already widely in use and will become perhaps incredibly more so as we put science to our humanitarian uses."

"IT IS THE SOURCE OF PUBLIC INFORMATION AND what we say to these massive receptive audiences which pose the problems and the challenges of our time."

"ALL OF US WHO USE THE IMPLEMENTS of mass communications have tremendous responsibility to utilize them more fully in the interest of common humanity in the light of present world conditions."

"IT IS A CURIOUS THING
THAT THE MORE the world
shrinks because of electronic
communications, the more limitless
becomes the province of the
storytelling entertainer."

"I BELIEVE IN
BEING AN INNOVATOR."

"YOU HATE TO REPEAT YOURSELF. I don't like to make sequels to my pictures. I like to take a new thing and develop something, a new concept."

ON AUDIO-ANIMATRONICS FIGURES:

"IT'S JUST ANOTHER DIMENSION IN THE animation we have been doing all our life."

CHAPTER 15

on television

"OUR CONTRIBUTION TO TELEVISION IS ENTERTAINMENT, created without deviation from our conception of what entertainment should be."

"AGAIN, WE FEEL, THERE IS A STRONG SECONDARY VALUE HERE— in that watching the Mouseketeers and their guests in action, boys and girls in homes throughout the land will feel impelled to discover and develop their own talents, whatever they may be."

"MANY TIMES RECENTLY WE HAVE BEEN ASKED THIS QUESTION: What is the difference in technique between TV and motion-picture production at The Walt Disney Studios? The answer to that, except in the theatrical use of CinemaScope, there is no appreciable difference. We go through the same motions. There are just many more of them when you produce for the two media."

"TELEVISION BEGAN TO MOVE
AND I BEGAN TO THINK ABOUT IT.
I talked to a lot of these television
executives and they said, 'What are you
going to do? If you go on television, what
are you going to do?' I said, 'I don't know.
I presume I'll do what I've been doing
all my life.' They said, 'Well, television
is different, you've got to do something
different.' I said, 'Well, I know, but I don't
think that the audience is any different.'"

"WHEN IT CAME TO TELEVISION, THE ONE THING I WANTED was to control my product. I didn't want anybody else to have it. I wanted to control the format and what I did with it. Now I have complete control, there is nobody that can tell me 'yes' or 'no.' I have it and if I fall down it's me, there's no one else to blame."

"EVERY TIME I'D GET TO THINKING OF TELEVISION I WOULD think of this park. And I knew that if I did anything like the park that I would have some kind of a medium like television to let the people know about it. So I said, 'Well, here's the way I'll get my park going. It's natural for me to tie in with my television.' So it happened that I had sort of say whether we went into television or not. I had a contract that said I had complete say of what we produced. So I just sort of insisted that my Disneyland Park be a part of my television show."

"TELEVISION AND THE CHANGES IT HAS BROUGHT ABOUT in the motion picture industry has provided an exciting new stimulus to our creative efforts. We are now able to work closer to the entertainment appetite of the public—much closer than when most of our production was animation and had to be planned in anticipation of the public's moods and market conditions well in the future. This change of pace has been very good for us, I believe, and our whole organization has gained in versatility and efficiency because of it."

"**I HAVE MORE LATITUDE IN TELEVISION THAN I EVER HAD BEFORE.** When I have an idea for something I have to then go and try to sell it to the distributors, to the theater men, and everything else. But television, I just get my gang together and if we think it will be something interesting, I say, 'Let's do it.' And I go directly to my public."

"**THROUGH TELEVISION I CAN REACH MY AUDIENCE.** I can talk to my audience. They are the audience that wants to see my pictures."

"THERE'S A BIG EXCITING PERIOD AHEAD OF US, and I say it's television. Television is an open sesame to many things. I don't have to worry about going out and selling the theater man. I mean, I go right to the audience. I have a chance by getting there twenty-six times every year. I have a chance to have a pretty good batting average and not have to get in a rut."

"INSTEAD OF CONSIDERING TV A RIVAL, WHEN I SAW IT, I said, 'I can use that; I want to be a part of it.'"

"TELEVISION IS OPENING NEW AVENUES FOR ME. You see, it's giving me new freedom, a freedom of producing things I feel we can do well, rather than having to hew down the lines of some title that somebody thinks is a prestige story . . . that the distribution people feel will sell, but maybe it is a bad story for us to fool with."

"**EVERY MOTION PICTURE EXECUTIVE,** whether in the production or exhibition division of our industry, must be aware that television today should command our utmost respect as a medium for exploiting our wares. To ignore what is a very obvious fact is to discount one of the greatest promotional channels ever put at our disposal to reach potential box office patrons."

"WE HAVE ALWAYS TRIED TO BRING MOVIEGOERS as close as possible to audience participation in our entertainment—to a feeling of intimate relationship with our cartoon characters. In Disneyland, people can actually take part in visible, touchable, moving and dimensionable fantasy. They can ride on it, fly with it, measure imagination with it and glean information from it about the past, the present and conjectional future. Thus our world in miniature becomes not only a valid source for a television program but virtually a must in what I regard as an obligation to our steadfast audience within reach of the telecast."

"THE GROWTH OF TELEVISION AS A MEDIUM OF mass communication among people around the earth cannot be halted, nor much longer delayed. And eventually every land will want to share in this international audiovisual exchange of ideas, of pleasurable entertainment and closer neighborliness."

"OKAY, MISS TINK—
on with the show."

CHAPTER 16

on enlightenment, exploration, and experimentation

"AND OUT OF OUR YEARS OF EXPERIMENTING and experience we learned one basic thing about bringing pleasure and knowledge to people of all ages and conditions which goes to the very roots of public communication. That is this—the power of relating facts, as well as fables, in story form."

"I'M JUST VERY CURIOUS—GOT TO FIND OUT WHAT MAKES things tick—and I've always liked working with my hands; my father was a carpenter. I even apprenticed to my own machine shop here and learned the trade. Since my outlook and attitudes are ingrained throughout our organization, all our people have this curiosity; it keeps us moving forward, exploring, experimenting, opening new doors."

"THE SPAN OF YEARS HAS NOT MUCH ALTERED my fundamental ideas about mass amusement. Experience has merely perfected the style and the method and the techniques of presentation. My entertainment credo has not changed a whit. Strong combat and soft satire are in our story cores. Virtue triumphs over wickedness in our fables. Tyrannical bullies are routed or conquered by our good little people, human or animal. Basic morality is always deeply implicit in our screen legends. But they are never sappy or namby-pamby. And they never prate or preach. All are pitched towards the happy and satisfactory ending. There is no cynicism in me and there is none allowed in our work."

"I AM INTERESTED IN ENTERTAINING PEOPLE, in bringing pleasure, particularly laughter, to others, rather than being concerned with 'expressing' myself with obscure creative impressions."

"SINCE THE BEGINNING OF MANKIND, the fable-tellers have not only given us entertainment but a kind of wisdom, humor, and understanding that, like all true art, remains imperishable through the ages."

259

"**EVER SINCE THE BEGINNING OF WISDOM,** man has been fashioning a brighter light and a stronger glass to help him probe deeper and deeper into the marvels of nature's secret world. Today, with the modern microscope, we can peer into dark corners we've never seen before. Often we can't explain what we see, but just looking is always a dramatic and thrilling experience."

"I CAN NEVER STAND STILL.
I MUST EXPLORE AND EXPERIMENT.
I am never satisfied with my work.
I resent the limitations of my
own imagination."

"YOU KNOW, THERE WAS ONCE
A TIME, and it wasn't too many
years ago either, when any boy who
was figuring on running away from
home just naturally started dreaming
about joining a circus."

"**THERE ARE FASHIONS IN READING, EVEN IN THINKING.** You don't have to follow them unless you want to. On the other hand, watch out! Don't stick too closely to your favorite subject. That would keep you from adventuring into other fields. It's silly to build a wall around your interests."

"YOU GET IN, WE CALL THEM 'GAG SESSIONS.' We get in there and toss ideas around. And we throw them in and put all the minds together and come up with something and say a little prayer and open it and hope it will go."

"INSPIRATION FOR WHAT WE PRODUCE IN TELEVISION and motion pictures comes from reading, observing the world of humans around us and also the animal kingdom."

"IDEAS COME FROM CURIOSITY. WHEN I SETTLE ONE IDEA, my confidence takes command; nothing can shake it, and I am constant to it until it becomes a reality. Then I drop it abruptly, and I rarely mention it again."

"I USE THE WHOLE PLANT FOR IDEAS. If the janitor has a good idea, I'd use it."

"WE HAVE TAKEN A NEW LOOK AT OUR
WORLD OF NATURE and humans with the
questing cameras; discarding some ancient
myths and adding dimension to our scope of
interests in the minds and hearts of people. The
sciences, medicine, psychology and others have
taken their place alongside the arts, the romantic
and fantastic in common human interest. We
seek to estimate the future and its bearing on
our existence, as well as dwelling fondly on the
past or indulging escapist dreams."

"MOVIES ARE A MEDIUM OF EXPRESSION, SAY, LIKE A SYMPHONY ORCHESTRA. Or like a painter's brush and canvas. The brush and canvas have been creating and presenting pictures for hundreds of years, but I haven't heard anyone say that painting was old-fashioned and had reached its limits. It's the painter—and the movie maker— the artist and the entertainer who have to be considered—not the tools of their trade. Like painting or music, it's the ideas and the material that get onto the screen that's important. Moving pictures can be and will be new and fresh and exciting as long as there are ideas and talent in the world . . . and there's never been any sign that creative people are disappearing from the world of entertainment. What is needed in addition to the creative ability is courage—courage to try new things, to satisfy the endless curiosity of people for information about the world around them. Movies became popular because they found new forms, created new sensations and explored new fields of popular appeal."

"BY NATURE I'M AN EXPERIMENTER. To this day, I don't believe in sequels. I can't follow popular cycles. I have to move on to new things. So with the success of Mickey, I was determined to diversify."

"WELL, WED IS, YOU MIGHT CALL IT MY BACKYARD LABORATORY, my workshop away from work. It served a purpose in that some of the things I was planning, like Disneyland for example . . . it's pretty hard for banking minds to go with it . . . so I had to go ahead on my own and develop it to a point where they could begin to comprehend what I had on my mind."

CHAPTER 17

on life

"I HAVE NO USE FOR PEOPLE WHO THROW THEIR weight around as celebrities, or for those who fawn over you just because you are famous."

"CERTAINLY WE HAVE ALL HAD GREAT CONFIDENCE at one time in our lives, though most of us lose it as we grow older. Because of my work, I've been lucky enough to retain a shred of this useful quality, but sometimes, as I look back on how tough things were, I wonder if I'd go through it again."

"WHEN YOU'RE CURIOUS, YOU FIND LOTS OF INTERESTING things to do. And one thing it takes to accomplish something is courage."

"THE WAY TO GET STARTED is to quit talking and begin doing."

"WHAT MUST CONCERN US MORE THOUGHTFULLY IS SUBJECT MATTER. DIVERSITY. We must appeal to a far wider range of audience interest than ever before. We must prove to the whole new audiences, particularly our alert and curious teenager, that the movies and TV can compete for their attention with all the exciting prospects and activities of their daily life in a wonderful world of facts, of splendid dreams, of inviting experiences."

"THE ERA WE ARE LIVING in today is a dream coming true."

"SOMEHOW I CAN'T BELIEVE THERE ARE MANY heights that can't be scaled by a man who knows the secret of making dreams come true. This special secret, it seems to me, can be summarized in four C's. They are Curiosity, Confidence, Courage, and Constancy and the greatest of these is Confidence. When you believe a thing, believe it all over, implicitly and unquestioningly."

"I BELIEVE THAT
ENTERTAINMENT usually
fulfills some vital need and normal
curiosity for every man, woman and
child who seeks it."

"FAITH I HAVE, IN
MYSELF, IN HUMANITY, in the
worthwhileness of the pursuits in
entertainment for the masses. But wide
awake, not blind faith, moves me. My
operations are based on experience,
thoughtful observation and warm
fellowship with my neighbors at home
and around the world."

"FANTASY, IF IT'S REALLY CONVINCING, can't become dated, for the simple reason that it represents a flight into a dimension that lies beyond the reach of time. In this new dimension, whatever it is, nothing corrodes or gets run down at the heel, or gets to look ridiculous like, say, the celluloid collar or the bustle. And nobody gets any older."

"THE ONLY PROBLEM WITH ANYTHING OF TOMORROW is that at the pace we're going right now, tomorrow would catch up with us before we got it built."

ON IDEAS:

"I'VE GOT A LOT OF THEM. I HAVEN'T WORKED them out and I haven't proved them out. I carry ideas around in my head for a long time."

"I HAPPEN TO BE KIND OF AN INQUISITIVE GUY and when I see things I don't like, I start thinking, 'Why do they have to be like this and how can I improve them?'"

"I AM A PATIENT LISTENER, BUT OPINIONATED to the point of stubbornness when my mind is made up."

"LEADERSHIP IMPLIES A STRONG FAITH OR BELIEF IN SOMETHING. It may be a cause, an institution, a political or business operation in which a man takes active direction by virtue of his faith and self-assurance. And, of course, leadership means a group, large or small, which is willing to entrust such authority to a man—or a woman—in judgment, wisdom, personal appeal and proven competence."

"I ALWAYS LIKE TO LOOK ON THE OPTIMISTIC SIDE OF LIFE, but I am realistic enough to know that life is a complex matter. With the laugh comes the tears, and in developing motion pictures or television shows, you must combine all the facts of life—drama, pathos, and humor."

"NEVER GET BORED OR CYNICAL.
Yesterday is a thing of the past."

"I HOPE WE NEVER LOSE SOME OF THE THINGS OF THE PAST . . . I love the nostalgic myself."

"WHY BE A GOVERNOR OR A SENATOR
when you can be king of Disneyland."

"YOU DON'T BUILD IT FOR YOURSELF.
You know what the people want, and you
build it for them."

"**DEEDS, RATHER THAN WORDS, EXPRESS MY CONCEPT** of the part religion should play in everyday life. I have watched constantly that in our movie work the highest moral and spiritual standards are upheld, whether it deals with fable or with stories of living action."

"**I ASK OF MYSELF, 'LIVE A GOOD CHRISTIAN LIFE.'** Towards that objective I bend every effort in shaping my personal, domestic and professional activities and growth."

"CHRISTMAS IS BIGGER than all of us."

"I BELIEVE FIRMLY IN THE EFFICACY OF RELIGION, in its powerful influence on a person's whole life. It helps immeasurably to meet the storm and stress of life and keep you attuned to the Divine inspiration. Without inspiration, we would perish."

"NOTHING IS EVER BORN AFRAID . . .
YOUNG THINGS—human and animal, boy
or black lamb—have had no experience
with fear. They rely implicitly on parents—
on someone bigger and stronger than
themselves, to assure safety . . . on God
as they grow older and threats to
security multiply."

"ONE OF THE MOST INTERESTING
THINGS ABOUT HUMAN BEINGS is their
individual behavior; and sometimes, of
course, their misbehavior."

"TOGETHERNESS, FOR ME, MEANS TEAMWORK. In my business of motion pictures and television entertainment, many minds and skillful hands must collaborate. ... The work seeks to comprehend the spiritual and material needs and yearnings of gregarious humanity. It makes us reflect how completely dependent we are upon one another in our social and commercial life. The more diversified our labors and interest have become in the modern world, the more surely we need to integrate our efforts to justify our individual selves and our civilization."

"WE GET ADVANCE REACTIONS TO OUR MOVIES AT previews and if the woman's reaction is good, I feel fine. If it is adverse, I begin to worry. I feel women are more honest about this than men. The men are more sentimental in one way—that is, they will sit there with tears streaming down their faces and will then come out and say '*Mfff.*' They won't admit it, because they are more cynical or shy or think it unmanly to show their sentiment. But the children, of course, are the most honest of all."

"ALWAYS, AS YOU TRAVEL, ASSIMILATE the sounds and sights of the world."

"IN BAD TIMES AND GOOD, I HAVE never lost my sense of zest for life."

CHAPTER 18

on health and wellness

"PHYSICALLY, DISNEYLAND WOULD
BE A SMALL WORLD IN ITSELF—
it would encompass the essence of
the things that were good and true
in American life. It would reflect the
faith and challenge of the future,
the entertainment, the interest in
intelligently presented facts, the
stimulation of the imagination, the
standards of health and achievement,
and above all, a sense of strength,
contentment and well-being."

"SUCCESS OFTEN DEMANDS A BIG PRICE. In my case it nearly ruined my health. The more successful I became, the harder I worked on new ideas, new developments, new techniques—until I reached a breaking point. Years ago I was close to a nervous breakdown. My doctor insisted I cut down to a five-day workweek, learn to relax, and get myself some hobbies which would release my tensions."

"WHY WORRY? IF YOU'VE DONE
THE VERY BEST YOU CAN,
worrying won't make it any better.
I worry about many things, but not
about water over the dam."

"IN MY VIEW, WHOLESOME
PLEASURE, SPORT and recreation
are as vital to this nation as productive
work and should have a large share in
the national budget."

CHAPTER 19

on love, kindness, and peace

"IN ORDER TO MAKE GOOD IN YOUR CHOSEN TASK, it's important to have someone you want to do it for. The greatest moments in life are not concerned with selfish achievements but rather with the things we do for the people we love and esteem, and whose respect we need."

"I HAVE A GREAT LOVE
of animals and laughter."

"BUT LOVE, THEY SAY, CAN
WORK MIRACLES. And a miracle
can make a story."

"WHEN WE OPENED DISNEYLAND, A LOT OF PEOPLE GOT the impression that it was a get-rich-quick thing, but they didn't realize that behind Disneyland was this great organization that I built here at the studio, and they all got into it and we were doing it because we loved to do it."

"TO ALL WHO COME TO THIS HAPPY PLACE: WELCOME. Disneyland is your land. Here age relives fond memories of the past . . . and here youth may savor the challenge and promise of the future. Disneyland is dedicated to the ideals, the dreams, and the hard facts that have created America . . . with the hope that it will be a source of joy and inspiration to all the world."

"DISNEYLAND IS A WORK OF LOVE.
We didn't go into Disneyland just with
the idea of making money."

**"THE INCLINATION OF MY LIFE—THE
MOTTO, YOU MIGHT CALL IT—**has been
to do things and make things which will give
pleasure to people in new and amusing ways.
By doing that I please and satisfy myself. It is
my wish to delight all members of the family,
young and old, parent and child, in the kind
of entertainment my associates and I turn
out of our studio in Burbank, California. I
think all artists—whether they paint, write,
sing or play music, write for the theater or
movies, make poetry or sculpture—all of
these are first of all pleasure-givers. People
who like to bring delight to other people,
and hereby gain pleasure and satisfaction
for themselves."

"DIRECT AND EASY COMMUNICATIONS—freedom of speech in all forms and its broadest sense—has become vital to the very survival of a civilized humanity."

"IN THIS MODERN DAY AND AGE, IT HAS BECOME imperative that we learn to get along with the fellow next door. Yes, this motto has more meaning today than ever before."

"AS I SEE IT, A PERSON'S CULTURE REPRESENTS HIS APPRAISAL of the things that make up his life. And a fellow becomes cultured, I believe, by selecting that which is fine and beautiful in life and throwing aside that which is mediocre or phony. Sort of a series of free, very personal choices, you might say. If this is true, then I think it follows that 'freedom' is the most precious word to culture. Freedom to believe what you choose and read, think and say and be with what you choose. In America, we are guaranteed these freedoms. It is the constitutional privilege of every American to become cultured or to grow up like Donald Duck. I believe that this spiritual and intellectual freedom which we Americans enjoy is our greatest cultural blessing. Therefore, it seems to me, that the first duty of culture is to defend freedom and resist all tyranny."

WALT DISNEY

Hollywood, California.

As the Christian world is celebrating the Nativity once again, the roar of the guns, the cries of the dying and the wails of innocent people are heard on the battle-fields. And an even greater holocaust threatens. Twice before in our time we have seen tyranny and lust for power thwarted by those who believe in the freedom of all mankind, only to see them circumvented in a brief few years.

In America, we have only one thought at this Christmastime, to pray that the world again be restored to a sanity that will insure all peoples the right to think and live as they choose, to respect the beliefs of all and to help humanity live a better life in the short span alloted to us on this earth.

In this aim we feel we are joined by all peoples who believe in the Divine Spirit. It is my sincere wish, in which I know I am joined by 150,000,000 other Americans, that we will be guided by the Supreme Being in restoring peace to the world, that all may live in hope and happiness.

To all peoples of good will, I extennd greetings of the Season.

Walt Disney

"WELL, OUR STORY PROVES THAT EVEN NATURAL BORN ENEMIES can become the best of friends under the right circumstances."

"A VISTA INTO A WORLD OF WONDROUS IDEAS, signifying man's achievements . . . a step into the future, with predictions of constructive things to come. Tomorrow offers new frontiers in science, adventure and ideals: the Atomic Age . . . the challenge of outer space . . . and the hope for a peaceful and unified world."

CHAPTER 20

on wonder

"NOTHING IN A LIFETIME OF PICTURE MAKING has been more exciting and personally satisfactory than delving into the wonders, the mysteries, the magnificent commonplaces of life around us and passing them on via the screen."

"THE MOTION PICTURE HAS BECOME ONE OF THE MARVELS OF ALL TIME; a true Wonder of the World in its magical powers. But what it has brought on the screen for every man and his family to see and ponder has been even more wonderful."

"FUN AND WONDER ARE THE IMPORTANT ELEMENTS, in addition to quality in production and performance, which are most responsible for the success of Disney productions. Fun in the sense of cheerful reaction—the appeal to love of laughter. Wonder in that we appeal to the constant wonder in men's minds, which is stimulated by imagination."

"IT ALL BEGINS WITH DREAMS."

"I THINK WHAT I WANT
DISNEYLAND TO BE most of all
is a happy place—a place where
adults and children can experience
together some of the wonders of life,
of adventure, and feel better
because of it."

"PEOPLE OFTEN ASK ME WHERE
WE FIND OUR STORIES about
animals . . . and my answer is that
Nature herself writes them. The wonders
of nature are endless. Sometimes we can
recognize ourselves in animals—that's
what makes them so interesting . . ."

"THE IDEA OF DISNEYLAND IS A SIMPLE ONE. IT WILL BE A PLACE for people to find happiness and knowledge. It will be a place for parents and children to share pleasant times in one another's company: a place for teachers and pupils to discover greater ways of understanding and education. Here the older generation can recapture the nostalgia of days gone by, and the younger generation can savor the challenge of the future. Here will be the wonders of Nature and Man for all to see and understand. Disneyland will be based upon and dedicated to the ideals, the dreams and hard facts that have created America. And it will be uniquely equipped to dramatize these dreams and facts and send them forth as a source of courage and inspiration to all the world. Disneyland will be sometimes a fair, an exhibition, a playground, a community center, a museum of living facts, and a showplace of beauty and magic. It will be filled with accomplishments, the joys and hopes of the world we live in. And it will remind us and show us how to make these wonders part of our own lives."

CHAPTER 21

on gratitude and appreciation

"YOU CAN DREAM, CREATE, DESIGN AND BUILD the most wonderful place in the world ... but it requires people to make the dream a reality."

"IN THIS, OUR FINAL REPORT ON THE BUILDING of Disneyland, I want to pay tribute to the many studio artists, craftsmen and engineers whose untiring efforts helped bring this dream into a reality. Without their skills and imagination, Disneyland would not have been possible."

"MICKEY MOUSE, TO ME, IS A SYMBOL OF INDEPENDENCE. He was a means to an end. He popped out of my mind onto a drawing pad twenty years ago on a train ride from Manhattan to Hollywood at a time when the business fortunes of my brother Roy and myself were at lowest ebb and disaster seemed right around the corner. Born of necessity, the little fellow literally freed us of immediate worry. He provided the means for expanding our organization to its present dimensions and for extending the medium of cartoon animation toward new entertainment levels . . . He spelled production liberation for us."

"WE'VE MADE A LOT OF FILMS,
AND WHILE THEY weren't all considered
comedies, I hope we've continued giving
you films that amuse, make you laugh, or
just keep you happy."

"I AM GRATEFUL TO THE WORLD
THAT HAS BEEN GOOD TO ME.
I try to be completely devoid of
snobbishness or pretention. This
might explain, at least in part, the
universal appeal of Disney pictures."

"WELL, MY GREATEST REWARD I THINK IS . . . I've been able to build this wonderful organization. I've been able to enjoy good health and, the way I feel today, I feel like I can still go on being a part of this thing after forty-some-odd-years of the business and also have the public appreciate and accept what I've done all these years.
That is a great reward."

"I HAVE ALWAYS THANKED GOD
THAT I ACHIEVED a certain amount
of success while my parents were still
alive—to justify their faith in me. It
meant so much to them."

"I SHALL NEVER FORGET AN AUNT WHO IS ASSOCIATED WITH some of my happiest and most exciting moments of boyhood. She too believed I was destined to become an artist. All through the years on the Missouri farm, where I drew horses, pigs and other domestic animals, and later in Kansas City where I went to grammar school, carried a newspaper delivery route and intended to become a newspaper cartoonist, she kept me supplied with artist's materials. Not only with paper and pencils and crayon colors, but most of all with praise and encouragement. Every time she came to visit us, every time I got a letter from her, became an unforgettable moment of my youth and had no inconsiderable influence on my later career as a motion picture artist and producer."

"TO BE WELL THOUGHT OF BY YOUR NEIGHBORS—the people who should know you best—is just about the most satisfactory thing a person can experience..."

"NO MAN ALONE CAN DO VERY MUCH OF consequence without the help of others..."

"I FEEL THERE IS NO DOOR WHICH, WITH THE kind of talent we have in our organization, could not be opened, and we hope we can continue to unlock these barriers as long as we are in the business of bringing a happy note to those who patronize our pictures."

"WE DEVELOPED SO MANY TALENTS AS WE went along that I lay awake nights figuring out how to use them. That's how we became so diversified. It was a natural branching out."

"DEVELOPMENT IN THE METHODS AND MECHANICS OF CREATING illusion through animation has been going on, as you know, for a long time. I can claim no part in its basic steps during the more than a quarter century in which I have been practicing its integrated arts. I can only pay my profound respects to the pioneers in the field of graphic fantasy—pioneers who brought a new medium of delight to the mind and the senses when the motion picture began projecting cartoons in life-like action."

"WE'RE ALL PROUD OF THE HONORS THAT MANY GROUPS around the world have given us. And we're even more proud that the public—whether in theaters, at Disneyland, or in their homes—continues to express its faith in the kind of family entertainment we produce."

"THE MOST IMPORTANT AIM OF ANY OF THE FINE ARTS is to get a purely emotional response from the beholder."

"BECAUSE THE EYE IS THE MOST SENSITIVE AND dependable of our sense organs, the motion picture offers the widest, direct avenue to our emotions. Whereas the still picture can suggest only a fragment of fact or fiction, the cartoon-in-motion is without limit in communicating ideas, events, and human relations."

"MORE THAN EVER, I BELIEVE IN THE PERMANENCE of any well-founded institution which recognizes and caters to the basic needs of the people, spiritually as well as materially. And in my opinion, entertainment in its broadest sense has become a necessity rather than a luxury in the life of the American public."

"A LITTLE MORE THAN TWO HUNDRED YEARS AGO a great essayist and poet said, 'The proper study of mankind is man.' It occurred to me that this might form the basis for an interesting TV program; you know, tell people all about people, their behavior, what makes them tick and so on."

"JUST RECENTLY I HAD THE EXPERIENCE OF rediscovering an interesting place down here in our studio basement . . . we call it the morgue. Of course, it's really a complete reference library of our motion picture history . . . but it's also kind of like an old trunk in the attic . . . packed full of things that remind you of times you remember . . ."

"WELL, HERE IT IS ANOTHER CHRISTMAS TIME, and I believe it's just about my favorite time of year. One of the nicest things about the holiday season is exchanging greetings with our many friends; for these messages, from all over the world, represent the true spirit of Christmas in many different ways . . ."

ACKNOWLEDGMENTS

THIS BOOK WOULD NEVER HAVE BEEN POSSIBLE WITHOUT THE COMBINED TOIL AND INTEREST of the entire staff of the Walt Disney Archives over the past five decades. We are immensely thankful for their dedication and that of their founder, Disney Legend Dave Smith and of current director Rebecca Cline. Their work is the foundation upon which much Disney scholarship is based and continues to inspire.

In this vein, particular attention needs to be paid to the Walt Disney Archives Research team, whose daily work in helping to preserve the written and informational history of The Walt Disney Company remains vital to the success of the department. With a tip of the hat, and wink of the eye (which would make Walt proud), this group is, quite simply, the best in the business: Nicole Carroll, Kevin M. Kern, Ed Ovalle, Matt Moryc, Madlyn Moskowitz, Francesca Scrimgeour, and Julia Vargas. We are grateful for your guidance, patience, and suggestions in refining this important resource as it took shape into this final form.

We're also grateful for the ace team at the Walt Disney Archives Photo Library, who provided extensive assistance and direction in selecting some of the new and fresh historical images found within these pages. To this end, we salute Holly Brobst, Mike Buckhoff, Maggie Evenson, Cesar Gallegos, and Heather Hoffman for their work in preserving this collection. The Walt Disney Archives Digitization team also offered key support in imaging and reimaging many of the photographs found within these pages, helping to ensure they appear as clear and pristine as the day they were captured. Thanks to Jeff Golden, Amy Opoka, Christina Pappous, Ty Popko, and Katie Strobel, we can present these images with all-new clarity. Additional—and vital—operational support across teams within the Archives came from Joanna Pratt and Kimi Thompson, who helped to keep us in lockstep along the way.

At Disney Editions, our editors, Jennifer Eastwood and Wendy Lefkon; designer, Lindsay Broderick; and managing editor, Monica Vasquez, helped to champion this project from the get-go, and we're lucky to be able to work alongside them. Ever the consummate professionals, they're also ardent supporters of Disney history, which routinely makes our jobs here in the Archives all the easier (and interesting) when they bring us new and engaging projects.

—The Staff of the Walt Disney Archives

BOTH THE ARCHIVES STAFF AND THIS BOOK'S PRODUCERS WOULD LIKE TO SPECIALLY THANK Margaret Adamic, Justin Arthur, Amy Astley, Randy Bright, Charlie Cain, Bob Chapek, Jonathan Chew, Jeffrey R. Epstein, Michele Fortier, Howard Green, Jesse Haskell, Jennifer Hendrickson, Brian Hoffman, Bob Iger, David Jefferson, Kiran Jeffery, Debra Kohls, Mark LaVine, Ryan March, Rose Motzko, Chris Ostrander, Paula Potter, Max Raley, Kristina Schake, Jeremy Schoolfield, Bob Schneider, Marty Sklar, Paula Sigman Lowery, Ed Squair, Dave Stern, Robert Tieman, Steven Vagnini, Michael Vargo, Cayla Ward, Juleen Woods, and the team at The Walt Disney Family Museum, especially Bri Bertolaccini, Kirsten Komoroske, Caitlin Moneypenny-Johnston, and Caroline Quinn.

ALSO THANK YOU TO THOSE AT DISNEY PUBLISHING: Jennifer Black, Ann Day, Monique Diman-Riley, Michael Freeman, Alison Giordano, Daneen Goodwin, Tyra Harris, Winnie Ho, Jackson Kaplan, Kim Knueppel, Vicki Korlishin, Kaitie Leary, Meredith Lisbin, Warren Meislin, Lia Murphy, Scott Piehl, Tim Retzlaff, Rachel Rivera, Carol Roeder, Zan Schneider, Alexandra Serrano, Fanny Sheffield, Dina Sherman, Ken Shue, Annie Skogsbergh, Megan Speer-Levi, Muriel Tebid, Pat Van Note, Lynn Waggoner, Jessie Ward, and Rudy Zamora.

SOURCES

Chapter 1

Page 2: Disney, Walt. Walt's Files (Publicity)—Byline Stories by Walt Disney, Folder 2 (WDA).

Page 3: Disney, Walt. Walt's Files (Publicity)—Byline Stories by Walt Disney, Folder 4 (WDA).

Page 4, top: Disney, Walt. Interview conducted by Tony Thomas, January 1959. *Voices From The Hollywood Past* [album], Delos Records, 1975.

Page 4, bottom: Disney, Walt. Interview for the Canadian Broadcasting Company. Conducted by Fletcher Markle, 25 September 1963 (WDA).

Page 5, top: Disney, Walt. Interview conducted by Pat McGuinness, "ABC Radio Portrait," *Personal Portrait*, 30 January 1965, KABC (WDA).

Page 5, bottom: Disney, Walt. *Wisdom,* Vol. 32, 1959 (WDA).

Page 6: Disney, Walt. *Wisdom,* Vol. 32, 1959 (WDA).

Page 7, top: Disney, Walt. Walt's Files (Publicity)—Byline Stories by Walt Disney, Folder 3 (WDA).

Page 7, bottom: Disney, Walt. Quoted in "Disney's Cinesymphony." *Time* magazine, 18 November 1940, p. 55 (WDA).

Page 8: Disney, Walt. Remarks according to *Fantasia* Story Meeting Notes, 08 December 1938, Los Angeles (WDA).

Page 9, top: Disney, Walt. Walt's Files (Publicity)—Byline Stories by Walt Disney, "Animation" folder (WDA).

Page 9, bottom: Disney, Walt. *Wisdom,* Vol. 32, 1959 (WDA).

Page 10, top: Disney, Walt. Walt's Files (Publicity)—Byline Stories by Walt Disney, Folder 4 (WDA).

Page 10, bottom, and 11: Disney, Walt. *Wisdom,* Vol. 32, 1959 (WDA).

Page 12: Disney, Walt. Quoted in "Walt Disney's True-Life Fantasyland" by Stanley Handman. *Weekend Magazine, Toronto Telegram,* 03 May 1958 (WDA).

Pages 13 and 14: Disney, Walt. *Wisdom,* Vol. 32, 1959 (WDA).

Page 15: Disney, Walt. "Showman of the World," 01 October 1966, National Association of Theater Owners, New York City. Speech (WDA).

Page 16, top and bottom: Disney, Walt. *Wisdom,* Vol. 32, 1959 (WDA).

Page 17: Disney, Walt. Walt's Files (Publicity)—Byline Stories by Walt Disney, Folder 2 (WDA).

Page 18, top and bottom: Disney, Walt. *Wisdom,* Vol. 32, 1959 (WDA).

Page 19: Disney, Walt. Quoted in *Walt Disney Productions Annual Report,* 1951 (WDA).

Page 20: Disney, Walt. Walt's Files (Publicity)—Byline Stories by Walt Disney, Folder 2 (WDA).

Page 21: Disney, Walt. Walt's Files (Publicity)—Byline Stories by Walt Disney, Folder 4 (WDA).

Page 22: Disney, Walt. *Wisdom,* Vol. 32, 1959 (WDA).

Page 23: Disney, Walt. Quoted in "The Wonderful World of Walt Disney" by Bill Ballantine. *Vista,* Vol. II, Winter 1966–1967 (WDA).

Page 24: Disney, Walt. Interview for the Canadian Broadcasting Company. Conducted by Fletcher Markle, 25 September 1963 (WDA).

Page 25: Disney, Walt. Remarks at *Fantasia* premiere, 13 November 1940, New York City (WDA).

Page 26, top: Disney, Walt. Quoted in *Walt Disney Productions Annual Report,* 1950 (WDA).

Page 26, bottom: Disney, Walt. *Wisdom,* Vol. 32, 1959 (WDA).

Page 27: Disney, Walt. "Showman of the World," 01 October 1966, National Association of Theater Owners, New York City. Speech (WDA).

Page 28, top: Disney, Walt. Walt's Files (Publicity)—Byline Stories by Walt Disney,

Folder 4 (WDA).

Page 28, bottom: Disney, Walt, host. "Tricks of Our Trade," directed by Wilfred Jackson, 13 February 1957. Aired on television.

Page 29: Disney, Walt. Walt's Files (Publicity)—Byline Stories by Walt Disney, Folder 4 (WDA).

Page 30: Disney, Walt. Walt's Files (Publicity)—Byline Stories by Walt Disney, Folder 3 (WDA).

Page 31, top: Disney, Walt. Walt's Files (Publicity)—Byline Stories by Walt Disney, Folder 4 (WDA).

Pages 31, bottom; 32; 33; and 34: Disney, Walt. *Wisdom,* Vol. 32, 1959 (WDA).

Page 35: Disney, Walt. Interview conducted by Peter Martin, c. 1956, 1961. Transcript, Reel 11 (Walt Disney Family Foundation).

Page 36: Disney, Walt. Quoted in "Walt Disney's True-Life Fantasyland" by Stanley Handman. *Weekend Magazine, Toronto Telegram,* 03 May 1958 (WDA).

Page 37: Disney, Walt. "Showman of the World," 01 October 1966, National Association of Theater Owners, New York City. Speech (WDA).

Page 38: Disney, Walt. Walt's Files (Publicity)—Byline Stories by Walt Disney, Folder 4 (WDA).

Page 39, top: Disney, Walt. "Why I Like Making Nature Films," *Woman's Home Companion,* May 1954, p. 38 (WDA).

Page 39, bottom: Disney, Walt. *Wisdom,* Vol. 32, 1959 (WDA).

Chapter 2

Pages 42 and 43: Disney, Walt. "Story of Mickey Mouse," *University of the Air* [radio program]. 13 October 1947 (WDA).

Page 44, top: Disney, Walt. Quoted in "Mickey's Career Epic One," *Exhibitors Complete Campaign for Walt Disney's Mickey Mouse and Silly Symphonies* [Publicity press book], United Artists, 1932, p. 34 (WDA).

Page 44, bottom: Disney, Walt. Quoted in "Newspapers Stories," *Join Mickey Mouse in His Lucky Seventh Birthday Party!*

[Promotional kit], 1935, p. 17 (WDA).

Page 45, top and bottom: Disney, Walt, host. "The Disneyland Story" (aka "What is Disneyland? / The Story of Mickey Mouse"), directed by Robert Florey, 27 October 1954. Aired on television.

Chapter 3

Page 48: Disney, Walt. *Wisdom,* Vol. 32, 1959 (WDA).

Page 49: Disney, Walt. Walt's Files (Publicity)—Byline Stories by Walt Disney, Folder 4 (WDA).

Page 50, top: Disney, Walt. Walt's Files (Publicity)—Byline Stories by Walt Disney, "Animation" folder (WDA).

Pages 50, bottom, and 51: Disney, Walt. *Wisdom,* Vol. 32, 1959 (WDA).

Page 52, top: Disney, Walt. Quoted in *The Art of Animation* by Bob Thomas, Simon and Schuster, 1958, p. 38.

Page 52, bottom: Disney, Walt. *Wisdom,* Vol. 32, 1959 (WDA).

Page 53: Disney, Walt. *Wisdom,* Vol. 32, 1959 (WDA).

Page 54: Disney, Walt. Interview at the time of *Sleeping Beauty* (1959) (WDA).

Page 55: Disney, Walt. "Deeds Rather Than Words." Walt's Files (Publicity)—Byline Stories by Walt Disney, "Religion" folder (WDA).

Page 56: Disney, Walt. Interview at the time of *Sleeping Beauty* (1959) (WDA).

Page 57: Disney, Walt, host. Written for "The Mad Hermit of Chimney Butte," directed by Jack Hannah, 01 April 1960. Aired on television.

Chapter 4

Page 60: Disney, Walt. Interview for the Canadian Broadcasting Company. Conducted by Fletcher Markle, 25 September 1963 (WDA).

Page 61, top: Disney, Walt. Walt's Files (Publicity)—Byline Stories by Walt Disney, "Disneyland" folder (WDA).

Page 61, bottom: Disney, Walt. "Disney to Build Futuristic 'World' in Florida" by Norma Lee Browning, *Chicago Tribune,* 25 October 1966. Also quoted in "Walt Disney

World Background and Philosophy" by Marty Sklar, 1967 (WDA).

Pages 62 and 63: Disney, Walt. Walt's Files (Publicity)—"Disneyland" folder (WDA).

Page 64: Disney, Walt, host. "A Progress Report / Nature's Half Acre," *Disneyland*, directed by Winston Hibler, Al Teeter, 09 February 1955. Aired on television.

Page 65, top: Disney, Walt. Interview conducted by Peter Martin, c. 1956, 1961. Transcript, Reel 11 (Walt Disney Family Foundation).

Page 65, bottom: Disney, Walt. Disneyland Tencennial Awards Presentation, 18 July 1965, Disneyland Hotel, Anaheim, California. Speech (WDA).

Page 66: Disney, Walt. Interview for the Canadian Broadcasting Company. Conducted by Fletcher Markle, 25 September 1963 (WDA).

Page 67: Disney, Walt. Disneyland Tencennial Awards Presentation, 18 July 1965, Disneyland Hotel, Anaheim, California. Speech (WDA).

Pages 68 and 69, top: Disney, Walt. Disneyland Press Clippings—Tencennial Publicity Book 2 (WDA).

Page 69, bottom: Disney, Walt, host. "Disneyland After Dark," directed by Hamilton S. Luske, 15 April 1962. Aired on television.

Pages 70, top and bottom, and 71: Disney, Walt. Disneyland Press Clippings—Tencennial Publicity Book 1 (WDA).

Page 72: Disney, Walt. *Disneyland* [prospectus brochure], WED Enterprises, 1953. Also quoted in "Walt Disney World Background and Philosophy" by Marty Sklar, 1967 (WDA).

Page 73, top: Disney, Walt. Interview conducted by Peter Martin, c. 1956, 1961. Transcript, Reel 1 (Walt Disney Family Foundation).

Page 73, bottom: Disney, Walt. Remarks at Florida Press Conference, 15 November 1965, Orlando, Florida (WDA).

Page 74: Disney, Walt. Interview conducted by Peter Martin, c. 1956, 1961. Transcript, Reel 9 (Walt Disney Family Foundation).

Page 75, top and bottom: Disney, Walt. Quoted in "Walt Disney World Background and Philosophy" by Marty Sklar, 1967 (WDA).

Page 76: Disney, Walt. "A word from Walt . . ." *Your Disneyland: A Guide for Hosts and Hostesses*, Disneyland, Inc., 1955, p. 1 (WDA).

Page 77, top: Disney, Walt. Quoted in *Art and Management of the Theme Show* by Van France, 15 March 1970, p. 75 (WDA).

Page 77, bottom: Disney, Walt. Quoted in *Walt Disney's Guide to Disneyland*, Souvenir Guide Book, 1958, p. 2 (WDA).

Page 78: Disney, Walt, host. "Holiday Time at Disneyland," directed by Hamilton S. Luske, 23 December 1962. Aired on television.

Page 79: Disney, Walt. Quoted in *Disneyland Dictionary*, 1959 (WDA).

Page 80: Disney, Walt. Adventureland Bronze Plaque copy [draft]. Written: 22 June 1955 (WDA).

Page 81: Disney, Walt. Fantasyland dedication, *Dateline Disneyland*, directed by Stuart Phelps and John Rich, hosted by Art Linkletter, Bob Cummings, and Ronald Reagan, 17 July 1955. Aired on television.

Page 82, top: Disney, Walt. Frontierland Dedication Plaque copy [draft]. Written: 05 July 1955 (WDA).

Page 82, bottom: Disney, Walt. Main Street Bronze Plaque copy [draft]. Written: 22 June 1955 (WDA).

Page 83: Disney, Walt. Interview conducted by Bob Wright, *KNBC Survey*, Recorded: 24 August 1966 (WDA).

Page 84, top and bottom: Disney, Walt. "Yesterday Tomorrow and Today," *Tencennial Souvenir Edition*, Newspaper advertising supplement, Disneyland, 1965 (WDA).

Page 85, top: Disney, Walt. Speech for Medal of Honor holders, 14 October 1966, Disneyland, Anaheim, California (WDA).

Page 85, bottom: Disney, Walt. "Disney to Build Futuristic 'World' in Florida" by Norma Lee Browning, *Chicago Tribune*, 25 October 1966. Also quoted in "Walt Disney World Background and Philosophy" by Marty Sklar, 1967 (WDA).

Page 86: Disney, Walt. "Welcome to Disneyland," *The Story of Disneyland*, Souvenir Guide Book, 1955 (WDA).

Page 87: Disney, Walt. Remarks at Florida Press Conference, 15 November 1965, Orlando, Florida. Also quoted in "Walt Disney World Background and Philosophy" by Marty Sklar, 1967 (WDA).

Pages 88 and 89, top: Disney, Walt, host. *EPCOT* ("The Florida Film"). Filmed: 27 October 1966. Promotional film shown to Florida residents and leaders of American industry in 1967 to help outline Walt's ideas for EPCOT and what would become the Walt Disney World Resort.

Page 89, bottom: Disney, Walt. Remarks at Florida Press Conference, 15 November 1965, Orlando, Florida (WDA).

Page 90: Disney, Walt, host. *EPCOT* ("The Florida Film"). Filmed: 27 October 1966.

Page 91: Disney, Walt. Remarks at Florida Press Conference, 15 November 1965, Orlando, Florida. Also quoted in "Walt Disney World Background and Philosophy" by Marty Sklar, 1967 (WDA).

Pages 92 and 93: Disney, Walt, host. *EPCOT* ("The Florida Film"). Filmed: 27 October 1966.

Page 94: Disney, Walt. Interview conducted by Peter Martin, c. 1956, 1961. Transcript, Reel 9 (Walt Disney Family Foundation).

Page 95: Disney, Walt. *Tencennial Souvenir Edition*, Newspaper advertising supplement, Disneyland, 1965 (WDA).

Chapter 5

Page 98: Disney, Walt. Interview conducted by Tony Thomas, January 1959. *Voices From The Hollywood Past* [album], Delos Records, 1975.

Page 99, top: Disney, Walt. *Wisdom,* Vol. 32, 1959 (WDA).

Page 99, bottom: Disney, Walt. "Showman of the World," 01 October 1966, National Association of Theater Owners, New York City. Speech (WDA).

Page 100: Disney, Walt. Walt's Files (Publicity)—Byline Stories by Walt Disney, Folder 1 (WDA).

Page 101: Disney, Walt. Walt's Files

(Publicity)—Byline Stories by Walt Disney, Folder 4 (WDA).

Page 102: Disney, Walt. Quoted in *Walt Disney Productions Annual Report*, 1965 (WDA).

Page 103, top: Disney, Walt. Narration for *Total Image Presentation*, 1965 (WDA).

Page 103, bottom: Disney, Walt. Disneyland Press Clippings—Tencennial Publicity Book 1 (WDA).

Page 104, top: Disney, Walt. *Wisdom,* Vol. 32, 1959 (WDA).

Page 104, bottom: Disney, Walt. Narration for *Total Image Presentation*, 1965 (WDA).

Page 105: Disney, Walt. Remarks at Florida Press Conference, 15 November 1965, Orlando, Florida. Also quoted in "Walt Disney World Background and Philosophy" by Marty Sklar, 1967 (WDA).

Page 106: Disney, Walt. Quoted in "Walt Disney World Background and Philosophy" by Marty Sklar, 1967 (WDA).

Page 107: Disney, Walt. Interview conducted by Bob Wright, *KNBC Survey*, Recorded: 24 August 1966 (WDA).

Page 108: Disney, Walt. Quoted in "Walt Disney World Background and Philosophy" by Marty Sklar, 1967. Similar quote in: "Yesterday Tomorrow and Today," *Tencennial Souvenir Edition*, Newspaper advertising supplement, Disneyland, 1965 (WDA).

Page 109, top: Disney, Walt. Interview conducted by Peter Martin, c. 1956, 1961. Transcript, Reel 6 (Walt Disney Family Foundation).

Page 109, bottom: Disney, Walt. Walt's Files (Publicity)—Byline Stories by Walt Disney, Folder 4 (WDA).

Page 110: Disney, Walt. *Wisdom,* Vol. 32, 1959 (WDA).

Page 111, top: Disney, Walt. Mineral King Material, Press Clippings, Book 1, August 1965–September 1966 (WDA).

Page 111, bottom: Disney, Walt. Walt's Files (Publicity)—Byline Stories by Walt Disney, Folder 2 (WDA).

Page 112: Disney, Walt. Quoted in *Walt Disney Productions Annual Report*, 1965 (WDA).

Page 113: Disney, Walt. Interview conducted by Peter Martin, c. 1956, 1961. Transcript, Reel 8 (Walt Disney Family Foundation).

Page 114, top: Disney, Walt. *Wisdom*, Vol. 32, 1959 (WDA).

Page 114, bottom, and 115, top: Disney, Walt. Walt's Files (Publicity)—Byline Stories by Walt Disney, Folder 4 (WDA).

Pages 115, bottom, and 116, top and bottom: Disney, Walt. Quoted in "Walt Disney World Background and Philosophy" by Marty Sklar, 1967 (WDA).

Page 117: Disney, Walt. Narration for *Total Image Presentation*, 1965. Similar quote in: "The Magic Words of Walt Disney" by Robert De Roos. *National Geographic*, August 1963 (WDA).

Page 118, top: Disney, Walt. Walt's Files (Publicity)—Byline Stories by Walt Disney, Folder 4 (WDA).

Page 118, bottom: Disney, Walt. *Wisdom*, Vol. 32, 1959 (WDA).

Page 119: Disney, Walt. Quoted in "The Wonderful World of Walt Disney" by Bill Ballantine. *Vista*, Vol. II, Winter 1966–1967 (WDA).

Chapter 6

Page 122: Disney, Walt, host. "Beaver Valley / Seal Island," 14 January 1966. Lead-in written for television.

Page 123, top: Disney, Walt. Walt's Files (Publicity)—Byline Stories by Walt Disney, Folder 4 (WDA).

Page 123, bottom: Disney, Walt. Narration for *Total Image Presentation*, 1965 (WDA).

Page 124, top: Disney, Walt. Walt's Files (Publicity)—Byline Stories by Walt Disney, Folder 4 (WDA).

Page 124, bottom: Disney, Walt. *Wisdom*, Vol. 32, 1959 (WDA).

Page 125: Disney, Walt. Interview conducted by Peter Martin, c. 1956, 1961. Transcript, Reel 6 (Walt Disney Family Foundation).

Page 126, top: Disney, Walt. *Wisdom*, Vol. 32, 1959 (WDA).

Page 126, bottom: Disney, Walt. Quoted in "Walt Disney World Background and Philosophy" by Marty Sklar, 1967 (WDA).

Page 127: Disney, Walt. Walt's Files (Publicity)—Byline Stories by Walt Disney, Folder 4 (WDA).

Page 128, top: Disney, Walt. Quoted in "The Story Behind Snow White's $10,000,000 Surprise Party" by Miriam Stillwell, *Liberty Magazine*, 09 April 1938 (WDA).

Page 128, bottom: Disney, Walt. *Wisdom*, Vol. 32, 1959 (WDA).

Page 129: Disney, Walt. Walt's Files (Publicity)—Byline Stories by Walt Disney, Folder 1 (WDA).

Page 130: Disney, Walt. Quoted in "Walt Disney's True-Life Fantasyland" by Stanley Handman. *Weekend Magazine, Toronto Telegram*, 03 May 1958 (WDA).

Page 131, top and bottom: Disney, Walt. Walt's Files (Publicity)—Byline Stories by Walt Disney, Folder 4 (WDA).

Chapter 7

Page 134: Disney, Walt, host. Lead-in written for closing of "For the Love of Willadean, Part II—Treasure in the Haunted House," directed by Byron Paul, 15 March 1964. Aired on television.

Page 135: Disney, Walt. Walt's Files (Publicity)—Byline Stories by Walt Disney, Folder 5 (WDA).

Page 136: Disney, Walt. Interview conducted by Peter Martin, c. 1956, 1961. Transcript, Reel 9 (Walt Disney Family Foundation).

Pages 137 and 138, top: Disney, Walt. Quoted in "Walt Disney World Background and Philosophy" by Marty Sklar, 1967 (WDA).

Page 138, bottom: Disney, Walt. Walt's Files (Publicity)—Byline Stories by Walt Disney, Folder 4 (WDA).

Page 139, top: Disney, Walt. Interview for the Canadian Broadcasting Company. Conducted by Fletcher Markle, 25 September 1963 (WDA).

Page 139, bottom: Disney, Walt. Interview conducted by Peter Martin, c. 1956, 1961. Transcript, Reel 1 (Walt Disney Family Foundation).

Page 140: Disney, Walt. *Wisdom*, Vol. 32, 1959 (WDA).

Page 141: Disney, Walt. Interview conducted

by Bob Wright, *KNBC Survey*, Recorded: 24 August 1966 (WDA).

Page 142, top: Disney, Walt. Interview conducted by Peter Martin, c. 1956, 1961. Transcript, Reel 10 (Walt Disney Family Foundation).

Page 142, bottom: Disney, Walt. Walt's Files (Publicity)—Byline Stories by Walt Disney, Folder 4 (WDA).

Page 143: Disney, Walt. Quoted in "Walt Disney's True-Life Fantasyland" by Stanley Handman. *Weekend Magazine, Toronto Telegram*, 03 May 1958 (WDA).

Page 144: Disney, Walt. Interview for the Canadian Broadcasting Company. Conducted by Fletcher Markle, 25 September 1963 (WDA).

Page 145: Disney, Walt. Interview at the time of *Sleeping Beauty* (1959) (WDA).

Chapter 8

Page 148: Disney, Walt, host. Lead-in written for closing of "Kids Is Kids," directed by Hamilton S. Luske, 10 December 1961. Aired on television.

Page 149: Disney, Walt. Interview conducted by Peter Martin, c. 1956, 1961. Transcript, Reel 10 (Walt Disney Family Foundation).

Page 150: Disney, Walt. Walt's Files (Publicity)—Byline Stories by Walt Disney, Folder 4 (WDA).

Page 151: Disney, Walt. Interview on *Snow White and the Seven Dwarfs*. Conducted by Cecil B. DeMille, *Lux Radio Theatre* [CBS], 26 December 1938 (WDA).

Pages 152 and 153: Disney, Walt. Walt's Files (Publicity)—Byline Stories by Walt Disney, "Children and Peace" folder (WDA).

Page 154: Disney, Walt. "Deeds Rather Than Words." Walt's Files (Publicity)—Byline Stories by Walt Disney, "Religion" folder (WDA). Also quoted in *Wisdom*, Vol. 32, 1959 (WDA).

Page 155: Disney, Walt. *Wisdom*, Vol. 32, 1959 (WDA).

Page 156: Disney, Walt. Walt's Files (Publicity)—Byline Stories by Walt Disney, Folder 4 (WDA).

Page 157: Disney, Walt. *Walt's Files* (Publicity)—Byline Stories by Walt Disney,

"Children and Peace" folder (WDA).

Page 158 and 159: Disney, Walt. Walt's Files (Publicity)—Byline Stories by Walt Disney, Folder 4 (WDA).

Pages 160 and 161: Disney, Walt. *Wisdom*, Vol. 32, 1959 (WDA).

Page 162: Disney, Walt. *Wisdom,* Vol. 32, 1959. Also quoted in Disney, Walt. "Deeds Rather Than Words." Walt's Files (Publicity)—Byline Stories by Walt Disney, "Religion" folder (WDA). Similar quote in: *Mickey Mouse Club* closed circuit show, 23 September 1955 (WDA).

Page 163: Disney, Walt. Quoted in "Walt Disney World Background and Philosophy" by Marty Sklar, 1967 (WDA).

Page 164: Disney, Walt. *Wisdom*, Vol. 32, 1959 (WDA).

Page 165, top: Disney, Walt. Remarks during *Mickey Mouse Club* closed circuit show, 23 September 1955 (WDA).

Page 165, bottom: Disney, Walt. Quoted in "Walt Disney World Background and Philosophy" by Marty Sklar, 1967 (WDA).

Page 166: Disney, Walt. Interview for the Canadian Broadcasting Company. Conducted by Fletcher Markle, 25 September 1963 (WDA).

Page 167: Disney, Walt. *Wisdom*, Vol. 32, 1959 (WDA).

Page 168, top and bottom: Disney, Walt. Walt's Files (Publicity)—Byline Stories by Walt Disney, Folder 4 (WDA).

Page 169, top: Disney, Walt. Quoted in "Walt Disney's True-Life Fantasyland" by Stanley Handman. *Weekend Magazine, Toronto Telegram*, 03 May 1958. Also quoted in *Wisdom*, Vol. 32, 1959 (WDA).

Page 169, bottom: Disney, Walt. Quoted in "Walt Disney World Background and Philosophy" by Marty Sklar, 1967 (WDA).

Page 170: Disney, Walt. "Newspaperboys— Ah, How Well I Remember!" *Family Weekly*, 15 October 1961 (WDA).

Page 171, top: Disney, Walt. Interview conducted by Peter Martin, c. 1956, 1961. Transcript, Reel 1 (Walt Disney Family Foundation).

Page 171, bottom: Disney, Walt. Quoted in "The Wonderful World of Walt Disney" by Bill Ballantine. *Vista*, Vol. II, Winter

1966–1967 (WDA).

Chapter 9
Page 174, top: Disney, Walt. Remarks at Florida Press Conference, 15 November 1965, Orlando, Florida (WDA).

Page 174, bottom: Disney, Walt. Walt's Files (Publicity)—Byline Stories by Walt Disney, Folder 4 (WDA).

Page 175: Disney, Walt. Quoted in *Walt Disney Productions Annual Report*, 1965 (WDA).

Page 176, top: Disney, Walt. Quoted in "Walt Disney's True-Life Fantasyland" by Stanley Handman. *Weekend Magazine, Toronto Telegram*, 03 May 1958 (WDA).

Page 176, bottom: Disney, Walt. Interview on the re-release of *Bambi*. Conducted by Dick Strout, 16 March 1966 (WDA).

Page 177: Disney, Walt. Walt's Files (Publicity)—Byline Stories by Walt Disney, Folder 2 (WDA).

Chapter 10
Page 180: Disney, Walt. *Wisdom*, Vol. 32, 1959 (WDA).

Page 181, top: Disney, Walt. Walt's Files (Publicity)—Byline Stories by Walt Disney, Folder 4 (WDA).

Page 181, bottom: Disney, Walt. *Wisdom*, Vol. 32, 1959 (WDA).

Page 182: Disney, Walt. Walt's Files (Publicity)—Byline Stories by Walt Disney, Folder 1 (WDA).

Page 183, top and bottom: Disney, Walt. Walt's Files (Publicity)—Byline Stories by Walt Disney, Folder 3 (WDA).

Page 184, top: Disney, Walt. Walt's Files (Publicity)—Byline Stories by Walt Disney, "Education" folder (WDA).

Page 184, bottom: Disney, Walt. Interview for the Canadian Broadcasting Company. Conducted by Fletcher Markle, 25 September 1963 (WDA).

Page 185, top: Disney, Walt. *Wisdom*, Vol. 32, 1959 (WDA).

Page 185, bottom: Disney, Walt. Walt's Files (Publicity)—Byline Stories by Walt Disney, Folder 4 (WDA).

Page 186, top: Disney, Walt. Quoted in "Walt Disney's True-Life Fantasyland" by Stanley Handman. *Weekend Magazine, Toronto Telegram*, 03 May 1958. Also quoted in Walt's Files (Publicity)—Byline Stories by Walt Disney, "Education" folder (WDA).

Page 186, bottom: Disney, Walt. Walt's Files (Publicity)—Byline Stories by Walt Disney, Folder 1 (WDA).

Page 187, top: Disney, Walt. Remarks during *Mickey Mouse Club* closed circuit show, 23 September 1955 (WDA).

Page 187, bottom: Disney, Walt. Walt's Files (Publicity)—Byline Stories by Walt Disney, Folder 4 (WDA).

Pages 188 and 189: Disney, Walt. *Wisdom*, Vol. 32, 1959 (WDA).

Page 190: Disney, Walt. Walt's Files (Publicity)—Byline Stories by Walt Disney, Folder 1 (WDA).

Page 191, top: Disney, Walt. Walt's Files (Publicity)—Byline Stories by Walt Disney, Folder 4 (WDA).

Page 191, bottom: Disney, Walt. Quoted in "Walt Disney's True-Life Fantasyland" by Stanley Handman. *Weekend Magazine, Toronto Telegram*, 03 May 1958. Also quoted in Walt's Files (Publicity)—Byline Stories by Walt Disney, Folder 4 (WDA).

Page 192: Disney, Walt. Quoted in "Walt Disney's True-Life Fantasyland" by Stanley Handman. *Weekend Magazine, Toronto Telegram*, 03 May 1958. Also quoted in *Wisdom*, Vol. 32, 1959 (WDA).

Page 193, top: Disney, Walt. Walt's Files (Publicity)—Byline Stories by Walt Disney, Folder 3 (WDA).

Page 193, bottom: Disney, Walt. Walt's Files (Publicity)—Byline Stories by Walt Disney, Folder 4 (WDA).

Page 194: Disney, Walt. "Rehabilitation Through Motion Pictures," *Builders of the World Ahead*, Report of the *New York Herald Tribune* Annual Forum on Current Problems, *New York Herald Tribune*, New York, 16 October 1944, p. 47. Also quoted in "Motion Pictures as a Medium for Rehabilitation," *Everybody's Weekly*, *The Philadelphia Inquirer*, 11 February 1945, p. 1 (WDA).

Page 195: Disney, Walt. Walt's Files

(Publicity)—Byline Stories by Walt Disney, Folder 4 (WDA).

Page 196: Disney, Walt. Walt's Files (Publicity)—Byline Stories by Walt Disney, Folder 3 (WDA).

Page 197: Disney, Walt. Interview conducted by Peter Martin, c. 1956, 1961. Transcript, Reel 12 (Walt Disney Family Foundation).

Chapter 11

Page 200: Disney, Walt. Walt's Files (Publicity)—Byline Stories by Walt Disney, Folder 2 (WDA).

Page 201: Disney, Walt. Walt's Files (Publicity)—Byline Stories by Walt Disney, Folder 4 (WDA).

Page 202: Disney, Walt, host. Lead-in for "Sing Out America" thirty-second television spot, 14 January 1966. Written for television.

Page 203, top: Disney, Walt. Quoted in *Souvenir of Mickey Mouse Club Circus* [program], Disneyland, 1955 (WDA).

Page 203, bottom: Disney, Walt, host. Lead-in written for "Toby Tyler, Part 1," directed by Charles Barton, 22 November 1964. Aired on television.

Page 204, top: Disney, Walt. Walt's Files (Publicity)—Byline Stories by Walt Disney, Folder 2 (WDA).

Page 204, bottom: Disney, Walt. Remarks during Freedoms Foundation at Valley Forge award ceremony presented by former U.S. president Dwight Eisenhower, 08 March 1963. Palm Springs, California (WDA).

Page 205, top: Disney, Walt. Quoted in "Walt Disney World Background and Philosophy" by Marty Sklar, 1967 (WDA).

Page 205, bottom: Disney, Walt. Press preview of the Great Moments with Mr. Lincoln attraction, 18 July 1965, Disneyland, Anaheim, California. Speech (WDA).

Chapter 12

Page 208: Disney, Walt. *Wisdom*, Vol. 32, 1959 (WDA).

Page 209, top: Disney, Walt. "What I've Learned From Animals." *American Magazine*, February 1953, pp. 22–23,

106–109 (WDA).

Page 209, bottom: Disney, Walt. Walt's Files (Publicity)—Byline Stories by Walt Disney, Folder 3 (WDA).

Pages 210 and 211, top: Disney, Walt. *Wisdom*, Vol. 32, 1959 (WDA).

Page 211, bottom: Disney, Walt, host. Trailer lead-in written to promote airing of "Niok" during *Walt Disney Presents*, 09 January 1959. Aired on television.

Page 212: Disney, Walt. *Wisdom*, Vol. 32, 1959 (WDA).

Page 213, top: Disney, Walt. Walt's Files (Publicity)—Byline Stories by Walt Disney, Folder 1 (WDA).

Page 213, bottom: Disney, Walt's Files (Publicity)—Byline Stories by Walt Disney, Folder 4 (WDA).

Page 214: Disney, Walt. Walt's Files (Publicity)—Byline Stories by Walt Disney, Folder 3 (WDA).

Page 215: Disney, Walt. Walt's Files (Publicity)—Byline Stories by Walt Disney, Folder 1 (WDA).

Page 216: Disney, Walt, host. Remarks for sixty-second sound-on-film television spot promoting National Wildlife Week 1966, National Wildlife Federation, 30 November 1965. Written for television.

Pages 217 and 218: Disney, Walt. Quoted in *Walt Disney plans for Mineral King* [promotional brochure], Walt Disney Productions, 1966 (WDA).

Page 219, top and bottom: Disney, Walt. Quoted in Mineral King Material, "Press Clippings, Book 1," August 1965–September 1966 (WDA).

Page 220, top: Disney, Walt. Quoted in "A promise from Walt Disney," *Walt Disney plans for Mineral King* [promotional brochure], Walt Disney Productions, 1966 (WDA).

Page 220, bottom: Disney, Walt. Quoted in "Walt Disney's hope for Mineral King," *The Disney plans for Mineral King* [promotional brochure], Walt Disney Productions, 1967 (WDA).

Page 221: Disney, Walt. Walt's Files (Publicity)—Byline Stories by Walt Disney, Folder 4 (WDA).

Chapter 13

Page 224, top: Disney, Walt. *Wisdom*, Vol. 32, 1959 (WDA).

Page 224, bottom: Disney, Walt. Quoted in "Walt Disney World Background and Philosophy" by Marty Sklar, 1967 (WDA).

Page 225, top: Disney, Walt. Walt's Files (Publicity)—Byline Stories by Walt Disney, Folder 4 (WDA).

Page 225, bottom: Disney, Walt. Interview conducted by Peter Martin, c. 1956, 1961. Transcript, Reel 12 (Walt Disney Family Foundation).

Page 226: Disney, Walt. *Wisdom*, Vol. 32, 1959 (WDA).

Page 227: Disney, Walt, host. "Cavalcade of Songs," directed by Wilfred Jackson and Peter Godfrey, 16 February 1955. Aired on television.

Page 228, top: Disney, Walt, host. Lead-in to "The Magnificent Rebel, Part I," directed by Georg Tressler, 18 November 1962. Aired on television.

Page 228, bottom: Disney, Walt. Quoted in "Mouse and Man." *Time* magazine, 27 December 1937 (WDA).

Page 229, top: Disney, Walt, host. "Disneyland After Dark," directed by Hamilton S. Luske and William Beaudine, 15 April 1962. Aired on television.

Page 229, bottom: Disney, Walt, host. "Tricks of Our Trade," directed by Wilfred Jackson, 13 February 1957. Aired on television.

Chapter 14

Page 232: Disney, Walt. Interview for the Canadian Broadcasting Company. Conducted by Fletcher Markle, 25 September 1963 (WDA).

Page 233: Disney, Walt. Special invitational showing of Great Moments with Mr. Lincoln for the Freedoms Foundation, 06 August 1965, Disneyland, Anaheim, California. Speech (WDA).

Page 234: Disney, Walt. Interview conducted by Dick Strout for W.E.D., *World's Fair Report*, Spring 1964 (WDA).

Page 235: Disney, Walt. "Yesterday Tomorrow and Today," *Tencennial Souvenir Edition*, Newspaper advertising supplement, Disneyland, 1965 (WDA).

Page 236, top: Disney, Walt. Walt's Files (Publicity)—Byline Stories by Walt Disney, Folder 2 (WDA).

Page 236, bottom: Disney, Walt. "The Language Everyone Understands—Communication by Motion Pictures." For *Voice of America*, c. 1959. Also quoted in Walt's Files (Publicity)—Byline Stories by Walt Disney, Folder 2 (WDA).

Pages 237, top and bottom, and 238, top: Disney, Walt. Walt's Files (Publicity)—Byline Stories by Walt Disney, Folder 2 (WDA).

Page 238, bottom: Disney, Walt. *Wisdom*, Vol. 32, 1959 (WDA).

Page 239, top: Disney, Walt. Remarks at Florida Press Conference, 15 November 1965, Orlando, Florida. Also quoted in "Walt Disney World Background and Philosophy" by Marty Sklar, 1967 (WDA).

Page 239, bottom: Disney, Walt. Interview for the Canadian Broadcasting Company. Conducted by Fletcher Markle, 25 September 1963 (WDA).

Chapter 15

Page 242, top: Disney, Walt. Walt's Files (Publicity)—Byline Stories by Walt Disney, Folder 4 (WDA).

Page 242, bottom: Disney, Walt. Remarks during *Mickey Mouse Club* closed circuit show, 23 September 1955 (WDA).

Page 243: Disney, Walt. Walt's Files (Publicity)—Byline Stories by Walt Disney, Folder 2 (WDA).

Pages 244, 245, and 246: Disney, Walt. Interview conducted by Peter Martin, c. 1956, 1961. Transcript, Reel 9 (Walt Disney Family Foundation).

Page 247: Disney, Walt. Quoted in *Walt Disney Productions Annual Report*, 1956 (WDA).

Page 248, top: Disney, Walt. Interview conducted by Peter Martin, c. 1956, 1961. Transcript, Reel 10 (Walt Disney Family Foundation).

Pages 248, bottom, and 249, top: Disney, Walt. Interview conducted by Peter Martin, c. 1956, 1961. Transcript, Reel 11 (Walt Disney Family Foundation).

Page 249, bottom: Disney, Walt. Interview conducted by Peter Martin, c. 1956, 1961. Transcript, Reel 1 (Walt Disney Family Foundation).

Page 250: Disney, Walt. Interview conducted by Peter Martin, c. 1956, 1961. Transcript, Reel 11 (Walt Disney Family Foundation).

Pages 251; 252; and 253, top: Disney, Walt. Walt's Files (Publicity)—Byline Stories by Walt Disney, Folder 2 (WDA).

Page 253, bottom: Disney, Walt, host. "From All of Us to All of You," directed by Jack Hannah, 19 December 1958. Aired on television.

Chapter 16

Page 256: Disney, Walt. Walt's Files (Publicity)—Byline Stories by Walt Disney, Folder 2 (WDA).

Page 257: Disney, Walt. Quoted in "The Wonderful World of Walt Disney" by Bill Ballantine. *Vista*, Vol. II, Winter 1966–1967 (WDA).

Pages 258 and 259, top: Disney, Walt. *Wisdom*, Vol. 32, 1959 (WDA).

Page 259, bottom: Disney, Walt, host. Lead-in written for "From Aesop to Hans Christian Andersen," directed by Clyde Geronimi, 02 March 1955. Aired on television.

Page 260: Disney, Walt, host. Lead-in written for reairing of "Searching for Nature's Mysteries," *Walt Disney's Wonderful World of Color*, 02 January 1966. Aired on television.

Page 261, top: Disney, Walt. *Wisdom*, Vol. 32, 1959 (WDA).

Page 261, bottom: Disney, Walt, host. Lead-in written for "Toby Tyler, Part 1," directed by Charles Barton, 22 November 1964. Aired on television.

Page 262: Disney, Walt. *Wisdom*, Vol. 32, 1959 (WDA).

Page 263, top: Disney, Walt. Remarks at Florida Press Conference, 15 November 1965, Orlando, Florida. Also quoted in "Walt Disney World Background and Philosophy" by Marty Sklar, 1967 (WDA).

Page 263, bottom: Disney, Walt. Walt's Files (Publicity)—"Questions Answered by Walt Disney" folder (WDA).

Page 264, top: Disney, Walt. Walt's Files (Publicity)—Byline Stories by Walt Disney, Folder 4 (WDA).

Page 264, bottom: Disney, Walt. Quoted in "Walt Disney World Background and Philosophy" by Marty Sklar, 1967 (WDA).

Page 265: Disney, Walt. Walt's Files (Publicity)—Byline Stories by Walt Disney, Folder 2 (WDA).

Page 266: Disney, Walt. *Movietime, U.S.A.* [radio program]. 31 October 1951. Speech; Walt's Files (Publicity)—Byline Stories by Walt Disney, Folder 2 (WDA).

Page 267, top: Disney, Walt. "Showman of the World," 01 October 1966, National Association of Theater Owners, New York City. Speech (WDA).

Page 267, bottom: Disney, Walt. Interview conducted by Dick Strout for W.E.D., *World's Fair Report*, Spring 1964 (WDA).

Chapter 17

Page 270, top and bottom: Disney, Walt. Walt's Files (Publicity)—Byline Stories by Walt Disney, Folder 4 (WDA).

Page 271, top: Disney, Walt. Narration for *Total Image Presentation*, 1965. Also quoted in "Walt Disney World Background and Philosophy" by Marty Sklar, 1967 (WDA).

Page 271, bottom: Disney, Walt. *Wisdom*, Vol. 32, 1959 (WDA).

Page 272: Disney, Walt. "A Production Viewpoint," *Independent Film Journal*, 01 June 1957. Also quoted in Walt's Files (Publicity)—Byline Stories by Walt Disney, Folder 2 (WDA).

Page 273, top and bottom: Disney, Walt. *Wisdom*, Vol. 32, 1959 (WDA).

Page 274, top: Disney, Walt. Walt's Files (Publicity)—Byline Stories by Walt Disney, Folder 1 (WDA).

Page 274, bottom: Disney, Walt. Quoted in letter from Joseph Reddy to Mr. W. P. Metzner, 08 January 1959, Walt's Files (Publicity)—Byline Stories by Walt Disney, "Religion" folder (WDA). Also quoted in *Wisdom,* Vol. 32, 1959 (WDA).

Page 275: Disney, Walt. *Wisdom*, Vol. 32, 1959 (WDA).

Page 276, top and bottom: Disney, Walt. Remarks at Florida Press Conference, 15 November 1965, Orlando, Florida. Also quoted in "Walt Disney World Background and Philosophy" by Marty Sklar, 1967. (WDA).

Page 277, top: Disney, Walt. Quoted in "Disney to Build Futuristic 'World' in Florida" by Norma Lee Browning. *Chicago Tribune*, 25 October 1966. Also quoted in "Walt Disney World Background and Philosophy" by Marty Sklar, 1967 (WDA).

Page 277, bottom: Disney, Walt. *Wisdom,* Vol. 32, 1959 (WDA).

Page 278: Disney, Walt. Walt's Files (Publicity)—Byline Stories by Walt Disney, Folder 3 (WDA).

Page 279: Disney, Walt. Walt's Files (Publicity)—"Questions Answered by Walt Disney" folder (WDA).

Page 280, top: Disney, Walt. *Wisdom*, Vol. 32, 1959 (WDA).

Page 280, bottom: Disney, Walt. Remarks at Florida Press Conference, 15 November 1965, Orlando, Florida (WDA).

Page 281, top and bottom: Disney, Walt. Quoted in "Walt Disney World Background and Philosophy" by Marty Sklar, 1967 (WDA).

Page 282, top and bottom: Disney, Walt. Walt's Files (Publicity)—Byline Stories by Walt Disney, Folder 4 (WDA).

Page 283, top: Disney, Walt, host. Lead-in to "From All of Us to All of You," directed by Jack Hannah, 19 December 1958. Aired on television.

Page 283, bottom: Disney, Walt. "There's Always a Solution." *GuidePosts*, June 1949. Also quoted in *Wisdom*, Vol. 32, 1959 (WDA).

Page 284, top: Disney, Walt. *Wisdom*, Vol. 32, 1959 (WDA).

Page 284, bottom: Disney, Walt, host. Trailer lead-in written to promote airing of "Square Peg in a Round Hole" during *Walt Disney's Wonderful World of Color*, 24 February 1963. Aired on television.

Page 285: Disney, Walt. Walt's Files (Publicity)—Byline Stories by Walt Disney, Folder 4 (WDA).

Page 286: Disney, Walt. Quoted in "Walt Disney's True-Life Fantasyland" by Stanley Handman. *Weekend Magazine, Toronto Telegram*, 03 May 1958 (WDA).

Page 287, top: Disney, Walt. Walt's Files (Publicity)—Byline Stories by Walt Disney, Folder 4 (WDA).

Page 287, bottom: Disney, Walt. *Wisdom*, Vol. 32, 1959 (WDA).

Chapter 18

Page 290: Disney, Walt. Walt's Files (Publicity)—Byline Stories by Walt Disney, "Disneyland" folder (WDA).

Page 291: Disney, Walt. Walt's Files (Publicity)—Byline Stories by Walt Disney, Folder 4 (WDA).

Page 292: Disney, Walt. *Wisdom*, Vol. 32, 1959 (WDA).

Page 293: Disney, Walt. Walt's Files (Publicity)—Byline Stories by Walt Disney, Folder 1 (WDA).

Chapter 19

Pages 296 and 297, top: Disney, Walt. *Wisdom*, Vol. 32, 1959 (WDA).

Page 297, bottom: Disney, Walt, host. Lead-in written for "The Pigeon that Worked a Miracle," *Walt Disney Presents*, 10 October 1958. Aired on television.

Page 298, top: Disney, Walt. Interview

conducted by Bert Reisfeld, 1965 (WDA).

Page 298, bottom: Disney, Walt. Park dedication, *Dateline Disneyland*, directed by Stuart Phelps and John Rich, hosted by Art Linkletter, Bob Cummings, and Ronald Reagan, 17 July 1955. Aired on television.

Page 299, top: Disney, Walt. Interview conducted by Bert Reisfeld, 1965 (WDA).

Page 299, bottom: Disney, Walt. Walt's Files (Publicity)—"Questions Answered by Walt Disney" folder (WDA).

Page 300, top: Disney, Walt. Walt's Files (Publicity)—Byline Stories by Walt Disney, Folder 2 (WDA).

Page 300, bottom: Disney, Walt, host. Written for "The Mad Hermit of Chimney Butte," directed by Jack Hannah, 01 April 1960. Aired on television.

Page 301: Disney, Walt. "Our American Culture," *Our American Way of Living*, 01 March 1941. Speech for radio series organized by the National Council of Women and broadcast during intermission of the Metropolitan Opera (New York).

Page 302: Disney, Walt. Letter to the world at the time of the Korean War. Prepared for United Press; Written c. September 1950 for use during the winter holiday season (WDA).

Page 303, top: Disney, Walt, host. Closing written for "The Hound That Thought He Was a Raccoon," directed by Tom McGowan, 20 September 1964. Aired on television.

Page 303, bottom: Disney, Walt. Tomorrowland Bronze Plaque copy [draft], Written: 24 June 1955 (WDA). Also quoted in Tomorrowland dedication, *Dateline Disneyland*, directed by Stuart Phelps and John Rich, hosted by Art Linkletter, Bob Cummings, and Ronald Reagan, 17 July 1955. Aired on television.

Chapter 20

Page 306, top: Disney, Walt. Walt's Files (Publicity)—Byline Stories by Walt Disney, Folder 1 (WDA).

Pages 306, bottom, and 307, top: Disney, Walt. *Wisdom*, Vol. 32, 1959 (WDA).

Page 307, bottom: Disney, Walt. Quoted in "Still Attacking His Ancient Enemy—Conformity" by Edith Efron. *TV Guide*, 17 July 1965 (WDA).

Page 308, top: Disney, Walt. Quoted in "Walt Disney World Background and Philosophy" by Marty Sklar, 1967 (WDA).

Page 308, bottom: Disney, Walt, host. Lead-in written for "Concho, the Coyote Who Wasn't," directed by Jack Couffer, 10 April 1966. Aired on television.

Page 309: Disney, Walt. "The Disneyland Story," *Disneyland* [prospectus brochure], WED Enterprises, 1953. Also quoted in "Walt Disney World Background and Philosophy" by Marty Sklar, 1967 (WDA).

Chapter 21

Page 312: Disney, Walt. Quoted in "May I Personally Welcome You to Our Disney Organization . . ." by Roy O. Disney, *The Walt Disney Traditions at Disneyland*, A University of Disneyland Handbook, Walt Disney Productions, 1967, p. 1 (WDA).

Page 313: Disney, Walt, host. "A Further Report on Disneyland / Tribute to Mickey Mouse," *Disneyland*. 13 July 1955. Aired on television.

Page 314: Disney, Walt. "Story of Mickey Mouse," *University of the Air*. 13 October 1947 (WDA).

Page 315: Disney, Walt. "Walt's Opening," *BBC Christmas Show*, 1964. Christmas greeting written for television (WDA).

Page 316: Disney, Walt. "From the Wisdom of Walt Disney." Walt's Files (Publicity)—Byline Stories by Walt Disney, Folder 4 (WDA).

Page 317: Disney, Walt. Interview for the Canadian Broadcasting Company. Conducted by Fletcher Markle, 25 September 1963 (WDA).

Pages 318 and 319: Disney, Walt. "A Moment I Can't Forget." Prepared for *Parade* magazine, 01 September 1955. Also quoted in Walt's Files (Publicity)—Byline Stories by Walt Disney, Folder 4 (WDA).

Page 320: Disney, Walt. "Man of the Year" citation. B'nai B'rith International, Beverly Hills chapter, Beverly Hilton, Los Angeles, 08 December 1955. Acceptance speech, Walt's Files (Publicity)—"Awards & Honorary Memberships," Folder 1 (WDA).

Page 321, top: Disney, Walt. Walt's Files (Publicity)—Byline Stories by Walt Disney, Folder 2 (WDA).

Page 321, bottom: Disney, Walt. Quoted in "Walt Disney's True-Life Fantasyland" by Stanley Handman. *Weekend Magazine, Toronto Telegram*, 03 May 1958 (WDA).

Page 322, top: Disney, Walt. Letter to be read at the Photographic Society of America Convention, New York City, 1953. Also quoted in Walt's Files (Publicity)— "Awards & Honorary Memberships," Folder 2 (WDA).

Page 322, bottom: Disney, Walt. Quoted in *Walt Disney Productions Annual Report*, 1966 (WDA).

Page 323, top: Disney, Walt. Remarks to John Culhane, 26 August 1951. Quoted in *Walt Disney's Nine Old Men* by John Canemaker, Disney Editions, 2001, p. 7.

Pages 323, bottom, and 324, top: Disney, Walt. Walt's Files (Publicity)—Byline Stories by Walt Disney, Folder 2 (WDA).

Page 324, bottom: Disney, Walt, host. Written for "Square Peg in a Round Hole," directed by Hamilton S. Luske, 03 March 1963. Aired on television.

Page 325, top: Disney, Walt, host. Written for airing of "Saludos Amigos," *Disneyland*, 08 January 1958. Aired on television.

Page 325, bottom: Disney, Walt, host. Lead-in written for a reairing of "A Present for Donald," *Walt Disney's Wonderful World of Color*, 26 December 1965. Aired on television.

Page 344: Disney, Walt, host. "The Disneyland Story" (aka "What is Disneyland? / The Story of Mickey Mouse"), directed by Robert Florey, 27 October 1954. Aired on television.

IMAGE CREDITS

Photographs courtesy the **Walt Disney Archives** and **Walt Disney Archives Photo Library** on the front cover and pages viii, 12, 20, 30, 38, 40, 46, 54, 64, 67, 79, 90, 94, 96, 105, 119, 120, 130, 132, 135, 146, 163, 172, 178, 190, 194, 198, 200, 206, 214, 222, 230, 232, 238, 240, 250, 254, 262, 265, 268, 275, 287, 288, 293, 294, 302, 304, 310, 312, 317, 318, 337, 340, and 344.

Concept artwork courtesy the **Walt Disney Imagineering Art Collection** on page vi.

Photograph courtesy the **Walt Disney Imagineering Photo Collection** on page 58.

Character artwork through book courtesy the **Disney Consumer Products Creative Design Team.**

PHOTO CAPTIONS

Page vi: Walt Disney Imagineering concept artwork for the statue of Walt Disney, installed at Dreamers Point in World Celebration at EPCOT. "It represents a more causal, approachable Walt, with no tie, and a very relaxed, informal pose," says dimensional designer Scott Goddard, Walt Disney Imagineering.

Page viii: Walt peers through the viewfinder of a camera on a trip to Berlin, Germany, 1958.

Page 12: Walt in front of the Animation Building on the Burbank studio lot with Mickey Mouse, Fiddler Pig, Practical Pig, and the Big Bad Wolf, 1964.

Page 20: Walt poses in a director's chair for the animated feature *Lady and the Tramp* (1955).

Page 30: Walt on the set of the live-action film *The Gnome-Mobile* (1967).

Page 38: Walt in front of story art from *Magic Highway U.S.A.* (1958) during production of the television show.

Page 40: Walt sitting at a desk with Mickey Mouse and Minnie Mouse figurines, 1930s.

Page 46: Walt as producer on the set of *The Sword and the Rose* (1953) at Pinewood Studios in the United Kingdom.

Page 54: Walt with plush dolls from *Snow White and the Seven Dwarfs* at the Burbank studio, c. 1940.

Page 58: Walt holds the Fantasyland dedication plaque in front of Sleeping Beauty Castle on the Opening Day of Disneyland, July 17, 1955.

Page 64: Walt views a model of the Primeval World diorama for the Santa Fe and Disneyland Railroad, c. 1965.

Page 67: Walt presents his bold plans for the "Disney World" and EPCOT projects in what would be his final appearance on film. Recorded October 27, 1966, on Stage 1 at The Walt Disney Studios in Burbank, California.

Page 79: Walt and a future Disneyland stagecoach on the Burbank studio lot, c. 1954.

Page 90: Filming Walt's television lead-in for the first episode of *The Saga of Andy Burnett*, "Andy's Initiation," 1957.

Page 94: Walt poses with an attraction model of the Carousel of Progress during the production of a promotional spot for General Electric, 1963.

Page 96: A studio portrait of Walt, c. 1949.

Page 105: Walt and then Bank of America chairman of the board Louis B. Lundborg during the dedication of "it's a small world" at Disneyland, May 28, 1966.

Page 119: A studio publicity photograph for the television lead-in to the film *Emil and the Detectives* (1964).

Pages 120 and 130: Note the embroidered Smoke Tree Ranch (STR) design on Walt's tie in these television production photographs. Walt signed the deed for a vacation home at STR—located in Palm Springs, California—in 1949. After years of enjoying their Coachella Valley getaway, Walt sold his vacation home in 1954 to help finance Disneyland. After the park proved successful, he moved into a second vacation home on the ranch in 1957.

Page 132: Walt arrives at the airport in Copenhagen, Denmark, for a European trip, c. 1964.

Page 135: Walt in front of a storyboard during the production of *Alice in Wonderland* (1951).

Page 146: Accompanied by dolls of cartoon stars from his then soon-to-be-released animated feature, *Dumbo* (1941), Walt grins as he enters his "working" office at the Disney studio in Burbank, California.

Page 163: Walt—with animator models of Goofy as well as Dumbo and Mrs. Jumbo and the Ringmaster from *Dumbo*—in his Burbank studio office, 1951.

Page 172: Left to right: Lillian, Walt, Diane, and Sharon Disney enjoying a family sightseeing day while in Paris, 1952. Also see page 342.

Page 178: Walt Disney is bestowed an honorary Master of Science degree from the University of Southern California, 1938.

Page 190: James Normile, Mrs. Nelbert Chouinard, and Dr. Clarence Thurber award Walt Disney an honorary Doctor of Fine Arts degree from the Chouinard Art Institute, 1956.

Page 194: Walt, accompanied by story artist Otto Englander, reviews storyboards for *Pinocchio* (1940).

Page 198: Showcasing a Civil War–era map of the United States, Walt records the lead-in segment for the second part of his television show *Willie and the Yank*, "The Mosby Raiders." Filmed on Stage 1 at The Walt Disney Studios in Burbank, California, August 24, 1966.

Page 200: Walt reading a *Pinocchio* storybook to his daughters, Diane and Sharon (left), c. 1939. Photograph by Earl Theisen.

Page 206: Walt during the production of a shelved 1964 television show known as "Pets is Pets," where he recounted the joys and practical needs of having pets.

Page 214: Historians point to many key points in Walt's life that fostered his true respect for animals and the natural world, including his work on *Bambi* (1942) in which Walt and his studio artists studied live deer.

Page 222: Walt sits at the piano in his formal office at the Burbank studio, 1941. On top are animator models from *Fantasia* (1940) along with a few characters that audiences would not see onscreen for years to come, such as Michael from *Peter Pan* (1953).

Page 230: Walt peers through a periscope while visiting the John F. Kennedy Space Center near Cape Canaveral, Florida, in 1965.

Page 232: Walt demonstrates Audio-Animatronics figures of the robin from *Mary Poppins* (1964) and a stand-in parrot from the Enchanted Tiki Room (still a new Disneyland attraction at the time) to Canadian Broadcasting Corporation host Fletcher Markle during an interview recorded in fall 1963.

Page 238: Walt with GARCO, the robot, during production of the television show "Mars and Beyond" (1957).

Page 240: Walt looks through a camera in this television publicity still.

Page 250: Television publicity photo for *Two Happy Amigos*, c. 1959.

Page 254: Walt and his family sailed from New York City on a trip across Europe from June 15 to August 6, 1951. One of their stops was touring a castle in Helsingør, Denmark, known as Kronborg.

Page 262: Walt pays tribute to Mickey Mouse in "The Disneyland Story," the opening episode of the *Disneyland* television series, 1954.

Page 265: In 1934, Walt was gifted a pair of wallabies, one of which is seen here with Walt and a large Mickey Mouse doll.

Page 268: Walt on set, 1958.

Page 275: Walt in front of a storyboard for "The Sorcerer's Apprentice" segment of *Fantasia* (1940).

Page 287: Walt dresses up for story time with his daughters, Diane and Sharon (right), c. 1939. Photograph by Earl Theisen.

Page 288: Walt rides a horse in full ranchero regalia, 1939.

Page 293: Walt aboard his one-eighth-scale steam train, 1952. The train's engine, *Lilly Belle*, was named after his wife, Lillian. He set up the hobby railroad in the backyard of his family home in the Holmby Hills neighborhood of Los Angeles, and dubbed it the Carolwood Pacific in honor of the name of the street their home was located on.

Page 294: Walt laughs on the set of a re-created studio office in this television production photograph.

Page 302: While the United States was engaged in the Korean War, Walt signed this letter to help spread a message of hope and peace during the then-forthcoming holiday season. Letter prepared and provided to United Press (known today as UPI) in the fall of 1950.

Page 304: Walt with a moon model used during the production of his "space" shows for the *Disneyland* television series, 1955.

Page 310: A studio portrait of Walt, 1949.

Page 315: Walt and his brother Roy in front of early production art for *The Jungle Book* (1967). The film was the last animated feature supervised under Walt.

Page 317: Walt posing with the first large shipment of Mickey Mouse plush dolls from Charlotte Clark, 1930.

Page 318: Walt's parents, Flora and Elias Disney, 1913.

Page 337: Walt examines a freshly printed Disneyland Records poster, 1963.

Page 342: Walt and his family enjoying a sightseeing day in Paris, 1952. Also see page 172.

Page 344: Walt—with a shadow of Mickey Mouse—at his Woking Way home in Los Angeles, California, c. 1932. Photograph by Tom Collins.

"I ONLY HOPE THAT WE NEVER LOSE SIGHT OF ONE THING—

that it was all started by a mouse."